SURVIVOR OF THE LONG MARCH

'I saw a column of 40–50 men and women coming round the bend. They were dressed in dark, filthy clothes that mostly hung off their skinny bodies ... It was a shocking sight. Their faces were white, their eyes sunk right in and they had no hair at all. I couldn't bear seeing this and my temper got the better of me. That red mist of anger, frustration, injustice and helplessness rose before my eyes. It was a bit silly, I suppose, you will probably say I was mad but I jumped out of that gully, scrambled up on to the road and rushed towards one of the guards. '*Schlecht*' – bad, I shouted. 'German culture, bad,' and I spat at the guard's boots. '*Schlecht,*' I moved my head down to spit again.

The guard hardly broke step and the next second, I felt the butt of his rifle hit me hard between my shoulder blades.'

SURVIVOR OF THE LONG MARCH

CHARLES WAITE

WITH DEE LA VARDERA

Foreword by Terry Waite CBE

SPELLMOUNT

Title page: Charles Waite on his return to France, 2010.

First published in 2012 by Spellmount, an imprint of
The History Press
The Mill, Brimscombe Port
Stroud, Gloucestershire, GL5 2QG
www.thehistorypress.co.uk

Reprinted 2012

British Library Cataloguing in Publication Data.
A catalogue record for this book is available from the British Library.

ISBN 978 0 7524 6519 7

Typesetting and origination by The History Press
Printed in Great Britain

Contents

Acknowledgements

It has been a pleasure and a privilege to help Charles write his life story. When we started in July 2010, I didn't really know if there was enough to fill a book. The more Charles talked, the more he remembered and the more interested I became. Little details were recalled which filled out the picture of his life. Events which had lain buried deep in his mind came to light; some funny, many painful. I thought that everything was worth capturing and recording for others to read so that people would know what he went through and understand what going to war was really like.

After many hours of taped interviews at his home (punctuated by cups of tea and slices of fruit cake) and then many hours on the telephone as I checked details and read chapters aloud to Charles for his approval, we achieved our goal. We laughed a good deal and shed a few tears as we journeyed together on this exploration into his past.

I couldn't have written the book without the help of family and friends (on both sides) and, in particular, those who provided family history, helped with research, undertook proofreading and checked language translation.

A special thank you to Terry Waite CBE for his foreword and to Peter Collyer for the map of Charles's route on The Long March.

Many thanks to: Allan M Jones; Vivian Smith; Jimmy Sellar; Robert Neville; Alfred La Vardera; Sue Richards; Adrian Scoyne; Barbara Summerfield; Gill Minter; Phil Chinnery at NEXPOWA (National Ex-Prisoner of War Association); Testimony Films; Manfred Schwarz at East Prussia Archive (Bildarchiv-Ostpreussen.de) and Albert Lipskey; Andrew Gladwell at Heritage Steamers; War Pensions, Glasgow; International Red Cross; National Archives, Kew; Imperial War Museum; Essex Records Office; Museum of London, Docklands and Ancestry UK.

Dee La Vardera
Calne, Wiltshire

Foreword

Although the surname 'Waite' is relatively rare I do not believe that Charlie Waite is a relative of mine although it is quite possible there is a distant connection. Whatever the case may be, we do have a connection of sorts. Charlie became a prisoner of war during the Second World War and I experienced imprisonment very much later in very different circumstances.

The Second World War is now fading from living memory and Charlie is one of the last generation who knew what it was to face the bitterness of that conflict. Many former servicemen have recorded their memories of those years and some have been published. It is important that we have a record if only to remind us of the futility of warfare. Yet Charlie's book does more than that. In the true tradition of the Waite family Charlie did not submit easily to his captors. On more than one occasion he showed his rebellious spirit which almost had him charged by the enemy with instigating a rebellion! Fortunately for him the charge was dropped and he faced a lesser accusation, thus living to tell the tale.

Charlie has told his story with a liveliness of spirit and a sharp wit. His book will take its place alongside many other stories of those ordinary men and women who in the service of their country gave so much that we might enjoy freedom today. Although it is often said that we never learn from history those who pick up this volume might take a moment to pause and reflect and recommit themselves to working for peace in today's troubled world.

Terry Waite CBE

1

Return Journey

I was glad my poor mother couldn't see me. A stinking, flea-bitten, lice-ridden bundle of skin and bones. A walking skeleton. Me, Charlie, her youngest son, nicknamed 'Bunny' because of the way I screwed up my nose when I laughed. But there was nothing to laugh about now on this hellish journey – the Long March. My long, long march back home from that God forsaken place in East Prussia where I had spent the last five years as a prisoner of war.

It was January 1945 when we left the camp with our guards, in one of the worst winters of the twentieth century with temperatures as low as -25°c. All I knew, it was bloody freezing and every bone in my body was aching from the cold and damp as we marched day after day, month after month, never knowing where we were going. Exhausted and starving, sometimes we pushed our way through snow up to our chests and walked on ice as hard as a steel bayonet. I walked blind, eyes screwed up against the icy winds. Hands burned with the cold, fingers clenched deep inside my greatcoat pockets.

Even though my feet were raw and bleeding, I was one of the lucky ones. I was wearing new boots sent by my mother. They were made from lovely soft leather and I had been saving them – goodness knows what for. Luckily, I put them on before leaving camp. I threw the old pair away soon after as I couldn't carry any extra weight. I remember I was wearing the leather belt a fellow inmate had made me out of the tops of discarded army boots. I had to keep pulling it in a few notches to keep my trousers from falling down, as I got thinner and thinner over the four months on the road.

We marched 10km, 20km, even 42km one day, whatever our German guards decided and the conditions dictated before finding somewhere for the night. Maybe some stables, a bombed-out factory or under a hedge. Sometimes we stopped for a few days to clear railway lines and bomb sites. More hard work, with little to eat or drink. Our stomachs hurt from hunger all the time. We were living on raw turnips, a handful of dock leaves, potatoes picked out from pig slurry, fish heads found in a dustbin, anything we could find or steal when the bread ran out. While the snow lasted we sucked handfuls to quench our thirst. When it thawed we looked out for a village pump, drank ditch water or did without.

How is one human capable of doing this to another? Hadn't we suffered enough as prisoners of war, forced to work all those years in dreadful conditions for nothing but watery soup, a crust of bread and a bed in a cowshed? Hating what we had to do, and powerless to do anything except obey orders; and afraid all the time of what might happen next. Keep your mouth shut, your head down and pray to get through it all and see your loved ones again.

At last we were on the move, heading west, we hoped, no idea of the route or the distance that lay ahead. We must have walked something like 1600km during those four months on the road before being rescued by the Americans and flown back to England. From East Prussia, north along the Baltic Coast, across Germany, huge empty landscapes and bombed-out towns, sometimes going in circles and coming back to where we started. Across the frozen river Elbe, south and then north, finally to Berlin.

No plan and no preparation for our evacuation. We left early one morning. 'Get your kit, we're moving.' We grabbed what we could: the remains of our last Red Cross parcel, clothes and our precious letters and photos if we could manage to carry them on us. The Russians were advancing so we had them to worry about them as well as the Germans and the Allied bombers above our heads. We were caught in the middle of it all. Nobody cared about us. We were still the abandoned, the left behind, the forgotten. I felt the same sense of fear and loneliness as I did on my surrender to the German Army five years before.

But I survived. Many did not. Men died of cold, exhaustion and starvation on The Long March. I remember helping to bury fellow men in shallow graves, those desperate enough to eat the black biscuits we found in an overturned railway truck and then died a horrible death. When I got back I couldn't tell anybody about what had happened during my years of labour in the camp. I was ashamed. I hadn't done any valuable war work or won any medals; I had no stories to tell of brave deeds; I just did my time.

How could I be proud of breaking rocks in a quarry 12 hours day or walking along miles and miles of rows of cabbages growing in muddy or frozen ground, cutting them off their stalks while watched by armed guards? Would my family have wanted to hear that I had seen a man beaten to death or a woman shot in the head while her baby was kicked along a railway line? They wouldn't have believed me and, anyway, everybody wanted to forget the war and get on with rebuilding their lives. So I kept silent about all this for nearly seventy years.

I know I am one of the lucky ones. I have always thought that throughout my life. Why didn't I die when we were under German attack on that road near Abbeville or as a prisoner of war under sentence of death for Incitement to Mutiny? Why didn't I simply lie down one night in the snow during the Long March and never get up again? Was it just luck?

Would life have been different if I hadn't passed my driving test at seventeen and there hadn't been a shortage of drivers in the Army? Would I have been fighting on the beaches of Dunkirk? I know that if I had reached there on that day in 1940, I wouldn't be here now. I am absolutely certain I would have been shot to pieces or drowned. It was a hot summer but we were wearing our heavy army greatcoats and big boots and had our rifles to carry. I never learned to swim so I would have just gone under the water and never have come up again.

So I was lucky not to be near the place. There were 8000 of our own troops killed, not counting the Belgian and French soldiers. A hell of a lot of people died in that area alone and this was just the beginning of it all.

Nothing can really prepare you for something like this. When I think of it now, there must have been something about me, and how I was brought up, that made me a survivor. More than just luck, perhaps.

* * *

My name is Charles Henry Waite, Charlie to family and friends, Chas to army pals – although only one of them is still alive. I was born in 1919, still in the shadow of the First World War, and named after my uncle. He was my mother's younger brother, a corporal in the Royal Horse Guards, killed in action in May 1915. We had a big framed photograph of him hanging in the kitchen in our small terraced house in Harpour Road in Barking, Essex. Uncle Charles looked grand in his smart uniform, holding his plumed hat in his hand, staring down at us as we sat at the kitchen table.

There were nine children and I was the youngest but one. When I was born Alfred, the eldest, was nearly thirteen, Marjorie, ten, Reginald, eight, Doris nearly seven, Leonard five, Winifred, four, and Muriel, nearly two. So by the time I came along my parents, William and Alice, already had their hands full with the other children as well as working to pay the rent and put food on the table. They had married young and family responsibilities followed quickly with the arrival of us lot.

Life was hard and finding and keeping a job wasn't always easy for my father. He worked for a local grocer but later, when he lost his job, became a bookie's runner. He wasn't unkind to any of us but he was never really close. With a large family and work problems he didn't take an awful lot of interest in me, and my mother just left me to get on with things too. She had a lot of extra work when Elsie was born in July 1920, because she needed special care. Elsie suffered from a condition known as St Vitus' Dance which meant she had fits and couldn't stop her arms and legs from jerking about. She didn't go to school and the symptoms disappeared when she was about fourteen. Unfortunately she went on to catch scarlet fever which left her with a weak heart.

So there was a lot going on at home. Half the time nobody noticed whether I was there or not. I loved going out in the morning to play in the park or ride my bicycle round town and I stayed out all day. When I got in late, often after teatime, nobody would ask me where I had been or what I had been doing. Maybe a hello, but they weren't bothered. Children were safe anyway in those days and I was happy exploring places and having fun on my own.

We lived in a three bed-roomed terraced house. Alfred and Reg, the two oldest boys, slept downstairs on mattresses on the floor and we all had to go to bed before they could settle down. My parents had the big front bedroom, the five girls were in another bedroom, which Leonard and I had to go through in order to get to our own little room. Eventually we moved up in the world – or so it felt like it to me. The change in our circumstances was brought about by a rather unfortunate incident to do with Alfred.

I was very fond of my big brother Alfred and he was more like a father to me than my own father. I looked up to him and he always looked out for me. I remember once going over to see Alfred and his family who lived 12 miles away in Grays. I was about 10 years old and I was meant to be going to Sunday School. On the spur of the moment, I borrowed sixpence from Muriel and walked all the way, turning up on their doorstep well after teatime. Alfred thought we ought to let the family know where I was so he went down the road to the telephone box to call father. Nobody at home had missed me and, as it was the school holidays, I stayed on there for a week. I had a wonderful time 'baby-sitting' my little nephew Roy. I would take him out in his pushchair to the park and round the town on little adventures.

I was very upset when Alfred lost an eye in an accident at work. He had been canteen manager for a few years at Dagenite Batteries Ltd which operated within the Ford Dagenham site and had been promoted to the production side when he was twenty-one. One of his men came to him one day and reported a faulty machine. Alfred went outside to check it and, as he was inspecting the machine which was attached to a wall, part of the mechanism, a sort of brush attachment, fell from the wall and hit him in the eye. He was taken to the Royal London Hospital in Whitechapel Road but they couldn't save his eye. He was eventually fitted with a glass one which was a very good match. I used to watch him, with a mixture of horror and fascination, popping the eye out to clean it and then popping it back in again.

So it was thanks to Alfred's compensation money from the accident, that my father was able to start a business in 1928: W. Waite & Sons, fruiterers, 99 Movers Lane. He rented a converted cottage next door to my mother's sister and her husband who ran a butcher' shop, and we, that is my parents, myself and the four youngest moved in. The older ones had married and moved out but came back to help in the business. I remember that Alfred was pretty good with his hands, working with wood and metal, and he constructed a nice front extension to the shop which opened out onto the forecourt.

The shop was open from 8am until 8pm six days a week with an earlier start if it was market day. Winnie and Marjorie helped in the shop and Alf and Reg worked on the delivery rounds. My father did the buying and went two or three times a week by horse and cart to Stratford Market in East London to collect the fruit and vegetables. He usually took one of my brothers with him and they left around 5.30am. Sometimes I went with them which I liked as it meant I got back too late to go to school.

The market was a huge place, rows of stalls on either side going on for ever, full of every variety of flowers, fruit and vegetables. The colours, the smells and the sounds were wonderful to a little chap like me. Some of the market traders were real Cockney characters, very funny. They used filthy language but they were honest and treated you well. We always gave sixpence to the porters who brought the goods out on huge barrows to the area known as The Island and loaded them on our vehicle. They weren't well paid by the stall owners so made up for it with tips.

As I got older I started helping out in the shop on Saturdays and in the school holidays. I didn't mind doing that because I was saving up for a bike and I got five shillings pocket money. And when I was fourteen I left school to work there full time. I didn't really have any choice about that.

The best days of your life, so they say, are your schooldays but not for me. I went up the road to Westbury Elementary School, a huge building which looked like a prison which, of course, it was to me. I was a nervous child, always afraid of the teachers, in particular Mr Milner. I can see him now, walking up and down the rows of desks with a cane in his hand, tapping it against his leg. If he asked you a question about something you had learned the day before and you had forgotten the answer, you got a rap on the knuckles. How did that help anybody remember anything? I've always hated bullies. Fortunately, when I moved up to the Juniors I had a different teacher who was more sympathetic and tried to encourage me.

I wasn't good at anything except drawing, which I loved. I was proud when my teacher pinned up a picture of mine on the classroom wall. Miss Davies thought I was a good artist and could go further but my father couldn't see the point of it. 'You can't make a living scribbling on bits of paper,' he said and that was it. The only time my father took an interest in me was when he wanted to stop me from doing something.

If your family don't understand you or don't have time for you, it's good to have somebody you can talk to. At school it was important to have friends; life was better if you had pals to play with and have a laugh. Friendship was a life saver during my years as a prisoner of war. I wouldn't have survived my time in the labour camp or on the Long March home without my pals – Jimmy, Laurie, Sid and Heb. You need people to share things with, to look out for you, to say 'Yes' or 'No, that's not a good idea.' There were a couple of occasions when they literally saved my life.

Ronnie was a school pal who lived in a little village down Barking Creek. There wasn't much to do there so Ronnie used to hang around my place and we would go and play in Greatfields Park opposite my house or go down to the quayside and watch the tugs coming up the river and throw stones at seagulls. During term time, he passed my front door on the way to school and, however early I was, he was there waiting for me and we would walk on together.

For some reason he always brought me food – a bit like my POW pal, Jimmy who was a gamekeeper before the war and a dab hand at finding eggs or stray chickens to supplement our meagre rations in our camp. Whatever Ronnie brought for his lunch, whether cheese or paste sandwiches, even a slice of cherry cake, he had some for me too. I don't know whether he had told his mother that I wasn't fed properly at home, but I would happily eat whatever he gave me on the way to school or keep it for later.

Sometimes, I told Ronnie to go on ahead because I had an errand to do for my mother and he certainly wouldn't have wanted to accompany me on that. I dreaded hearing the words: 'Charlie, can you drop this off at Grandma's on your way to school?' Unfortunately, I passed the bottom of Harrow Road where my mother's parents lived.

'Oh, no!' I said, 'not me, please.' I looked around for Win or Muriel but they had vanished. I hated going over there. I was afraid of Grandma Edwards who never had a good word for anybody, especially little boys.

Knock on the door, wait to hear the footsteps. Shuffle, shuffle. I knew it was Grandma because Grandpa was at the market. He was a farmer who had made his money during the First World War selling potatoes to the Army. Her first words were, 'Your cap's not on straight,' or 'Stop slouching.' She was always finding fault. She never said anything nice or that she was pleased to see you. Mind you, after having had 21 children, 14 of whom survived, I expect she was worn out by it all and didn't have any patience left for the likes of me.

I didn't like people telling me off or telling me what to do, especially at school and I couldn't wait to leave. I wasn't a scholar anyway. I remember when my father got into trouble with the School Attendance Officer, or 'Board Man', who used to go round people's houses checking on absent and truant school children. I had been off school for a while with influenza and had just had my fourteenth birthday in May. I was meant to go back to finish the term but I couldn't see the point and refused to go.

'All the other boys will laugh at me,' I said. When I saw the Board Man coming down Movers Lane or when Muriel spotted him first through the shop window she would warn me, 'Charlie, Charlie, Board Man's coming!'

I would run out the back and into the long storage shed where we kept the stock. I would get right down in the straw behind the sacks of potatoes and wait for the all clear.

This happened on a number of occasions and, in the end, my father got into trouble because he couldn't make me go to school. He had to appear before some of the Board people.

'You have failed in your parental duty, Mr Waite, to ensure your son's attendance at school. We have no choice but to impose a fine on you,' they said.

He had to pay up and to his credit my father never punished me or hit me. Many fathers, and some mothers too, were pretty free with the backs of their hands or with a slipper. You only had to look at some of the poor mites in my class, with bruises on their arms and legs, to know what they had to put up with. I was lucky that my father wasn't like that although he did believe in punishing his children. I remember Alfred telling me how dad had once punished Reginald for stealing.

Reg worked for a radio shop on the corner of Ilford Road and he rode a tricycle, like the ones used for selling Wall's Ice Cream. He used to deliver accumulators – the rechargeable batteries used by people who didn't have electricity. They were hired out to people for sixpence a week and Reg used to deliver them and collect the money. One day he decided he would not go back, ditched the bike and pocketed the money. The shop owner came round to our house in the evening asking after Reg but father didn't know where he was. When Reg finally turned up, he told my father what had happened and admitted that he had spent all the money. My father was furious and immediately went and repaid the shop owner the missing money. Reg lost his job, of course, and had to spend a night locked in our shed.

So I was lucky and got away without any punishment for truanting. Not going back to school until my birthday was my way of rebelling against my father. You're getting your way about me working in the shop, I thought, so I'll get my way about not going back to school. That evened things out between us.

What I really wanted to be was a policeman like my father's brother. I always had it in the back of my mind, hoping and praying that I would grow a bit more and a bit more every year. I knew that I wouldn't get to the right height so it was always going to be joining my parents in the shop. Times were tough in the 1930s and everybody had to pull their weight and my father expected me to do the same. So I left school at fourteen with no qualifications and started working full time as an assistant greengrocer in the family business.

One thing I hated was being out front, dealing with members of the public. I was nervous serving customers and preferred being out of sight, working out the back cleaning up, unloading vegetables into the separate storage bins for potatoes, carrots, onions and so on. I unpacked the fruit boxes and arranged them on display out the front before we opened up. I tidied up, swept and cleaned the floors. I didn't mind rolling up my sleeves and getting my hands dirty. For a short period we tried selling ready-weighed packs of vegetables which I bagged up in advance but people didn't seem keen on them. They preferred asking for 'a pound of potherbs' which meant a selection of different vegetables picked out for the stew pot and put in their baskets.

My parents liked to get away from the shop for a break and their treat was to take a tram up Ilford Broadway and go to the Hippodrome. Every fortnight or so, they would go to a film or see a variety show there. I was left behind to look after the shop when they went off to see the latest Fred Astaire and Ginger Rogers or Marx Brothers film. I was about fifteen and didn't mind being left on my own. I had my beloved Alsatian, Peter, for company so I felt happy and safe. He was a good friend to me and I was devoted to him. It was Reg who got me the dog from one of his customers. He was an unwanted pet, one of those Christmas presents which some kiddie had tired of. I could do anything with Peter. He always obeyed me and I was the only who could deal with the fits he had. When he died, I went out on my own and buried him on the marshlands.

I was always hungry, so when my parents went off up town, I enjoyed cooking up a little treat for myself. One of my jobs was to clean out the potato bins and I used to rummage through the contents looking for the tiny potatoes which collected in the soil at the bottom. I took them through to the kitchen, brushed the dirt off and washed them under the tap. I fried them up in a small pan on the stove in a bit of butter. Lovely grub.

Strange to think that ten years later I would still be hungry but this time literally starving, and eating potatoes again in completely different circumstances. I was trying to get home from Poland, walking all that way across Germany. In order to survive we had to look for food anywhere and everywhere. I remember searching an empty pigsty, desperate for anything to eat, and finding tiny potatoes in the filth and muck on the ground. I gathered them up, washed them in a stream and then cooked them on a piece of tin over an open fire in a bombed-out factory. Lovely, lovely grub.

Even though life was tough when I was growing up, there was plenty of food about. Our usual grocer was up at Blake's Corner but when Sainsbury's opened a new store in East Street in 1923, my mother shopped there too. I would walk up there on my own, clutching her grocery list. I thought it was the most beautiful place with its white tiled walls, shiny counters and uniformed staff. Its pyramid displays of tins and packets and the smell of ham and spices. I loved watching the butter men in their straw boaters cutting slices of butter off huge blocks. They slapped them into shape with wooden paddles, popped them onto the scales; they were always exactly the right weight for the customer.

I loved running errands, working in the shop and being on my own. I have always been of a nervous disposition and, to be honest, the war made me worse because I was frightened all the time. Frightened of what was going to happen to me and frightened of the awful things I saw. When I came home I found it hard to settle back into home life and the business. Everybody else had moved on with their lives but I still felt like the family errand boy and worse, I was afraid of my own shadow.

I have always been a hard worker, willing to learn. When you are on your own you have to pick things up quickly. And that is what I did and always have done. I was used to being around horses on the delivery round and I watched my brothers clean out the stables and put down bedding. When Alf and Reg were too busy at weekends to do it, they would ask me to go over instead. The two horses were kept at Harrow Road at the back of my grandparents' place. They were stabled at the side of the house in an outbuilding like a garage with big double doors, along with the two carts. Today you wouldn't be allowed to have a horse living right on your doorstop in a suburban street.

As I got more confident with the horses, I was allowed to take them one at a time to the blacksmith on the other side of town near the Quay. The first time I did this I arrived at the house and crept round the side and into the stables, trying not to make a noise. I opened the doors quietly and then moved the carts out. I didn't want Grandma Edwards to hear me and come out and give me an earful.

We didn't have a saddle so I got on the horse's back, put a halter over his head with a piece of rope attached and just went off. The roads were busy and buses and cars were trying to overtake and I got in a real mess every few yards trying to control him. The poor thing got upset at the honking and kept turning sideways, pulling on the reins. I was trying to keep hold of the horse and pull him back straight and it took me ages to get him to the blacksmith's.

The smith was waiting for me in the yard. He was a big chap with whiskers and dressed in a leather apron. I apologised for being late and told him what had happened getting across town. He looked at the horse, then looked at me and shook his head. 'Where are the blinkers? You've got to have the blinkers on?'

How stupid of me! 'They're in the stable,' I told him.

'Why didn't you put them on? The horse hasn't got anything over its eyes, poor wretch. Didn't know which way to go.'

'I never thought,' I said feeling very stupid. I never did it again. That's how you learn from your mistakes. So I said to myself, 'Charlie, you're fourteen. You're doing a man's job now. You'd better wake up and get things right in future.'

2

Always by My Side

When I was seventeen years old, all I wanted to do in life was learn to drive. I thought it was a manly thing to do. I didn't have proper driving lessons, well nobody did then, but I had a few lessons from a friend who worked for a haulage contractor. He worked nights helping the night watchman who did odds and ends like repairing punctures. They had a large fleet of lorries, all sizes and weights, and he taught me to drive on an old Standard car which had been turned into a truck. It had a gate-change gear box which was the world's worst to drive, never mind for somebody learning. Nothing like a modern gear box. You couldn't just slip it into gear; you had to double de-clutch which was really hard to do.

As soon as I had my seventeenth birthday, I sent off for a provisional licence. When I got it, Alfred offered to take me out in his rather clapped-out 10cwt black Ford van. There was a broken window in one of the back doors, no driving mirror on the left hand side, and no L-plates. On one occasion, Alfred had a bad thumb and decided to go home early from the shop back to Dagenham. His van was outside and I said jokingly, 'Come on, get in the van. I'll drive you back.'

And so I did. I got in and drove off fine, reached the top of the main road, turned right into Longbridge Road and then out of town towards Dagenham. It was dusk and I was driving along when all of a sudden I saw a policeman ahead, walking along the pavement on the edge of the kerb. He was wheeling his bicycle in the road and he turned round at the sound of our engine. He saw us coming, stopped pushing his bike, leaned it against a lamp post, stepped out into the road and put his hand up for us to stop.

As soon as I saw him, I pressed my foot down slowly on the brake and we came to a halt just in front of him. The policeman started to walk round to me in the driving seat.

'He's going to ask to see my licence,' I said to Alf. 'What am I going to do?'

'Just keep smiling, lad,' said Alf.

'If I show him, he'll see it's provisional. And we've got no L- plates.' I wound the window down an inch and forced a smile.

'Excuse me, sir. Do you know you've only got one front light on?' the policeman said. Then he walked round the passenger side front wing and touched the little light which decided to come on after all. He came back round. 'Oh, it's all right,' he said, 'must be a loose connection. But get it seen to as soon as you can.' We drove off and luckily we got away with it.

Now all I needed to do was to take my test, pass it and get out on the road legitimately before I got into real trouble and found my luck running out.

It was important for me to pass my driving test. I had never passed any exams at school and wanted to prove to myself that I was good at something. This was something for me, not for my father or my brothers. I wanted to get out on the road and be my own boss, at least for a little while, even if it was only going to market or delivering potatoes to another shop.

I had a few more lessons with my friend in his truck with the awkward gear box and then borrowed Alfred's van for the morning and went off by myself to the Test Centre in Romford. I was used to driving in and around Barking but there was much more traffic and different obstacles to negotiate in Romford. I was worried that I would get lost or take the wrong turning.

I met the examiner outside the centre. He was a very formal looking man, a bit like Neville Chamberlain, dressed in a dark grey suit and a black homburg hat. He checked my provisional licence and insurance before we even got in the van. As we sat inside, he asked me questions on the Highway Code and I had to show him I understood the correct use of signals. I wound down the window, put my arm out and did left and right, and up and down, as commanded.

When I finally drove off, he gave instructions such as 'Go straight on,' 'Turn right at the junction,' and 'Keep left here,' that sort of thing. I was keeping my eyes on the other cars and the bicycles, clutching the steering wheel while working out when to change gear. I was nervous and forgot that I was driving Alf's van and not the vehicle with the peculiar gate-change gear box and got a bit confused. What I did was to take my right hand off the wheel, lean across, nearly into the lap of the examiner, in order to get a good grip on the gear stick which is what I was used to doing.

'What are you playing at?' said the examiner and banged on the dash board with his clip board. I braked sharply and stopped and the examiner nearly hit his head on the windscreen. I apologised about my attempts at double-declutching and explained about the other vehicle. He looked at me a bit odd but said. 'All right, Mr Waite, you can proceed now.' That's it, I thought, my licence down the Swanee at the first attempt.

We went on a bit more until we came to a road which went up an incline. 'Stop,' he said. 'Hand brake on.' Then he got out of the van and disappeared round the back. What's going on? Now I'm on my own in the car. A couple of seconds later, he got back in and said, 'Pull away, please, and then stop on the hill.' I did as instructed and then he did it again – jumped out and went round the back. What he had done was put a match box behind one of the rear wheels so that if the car slipped back, when I was doing my hill start, he would know. Fortunately, he found the matchbox still standing up. After an emergency stop and reversing in the road he signed a bit of paper and handed it to me. He told me that I had passed.

Having my driving licence felt wonderful and gave me a real sense of freedom. Out on the road, window down, wind in my hair. This was better than roller skating behind the bus as it comes roaring round Ripple Road, down the hill and into Movers Lane. There's ten-year-old me, hanging on for dear life to the rail at the back of the bus, ducking down so that nobody can see me, as we sail past my house. Yippee! And letting go as the bus slows down at the corner and I come skating to halt outside the Park gates. Freedom again.

I had my driving licence now and I felt I could do anything although the reality was that I was very limited. I could drive my brother's van on my own and when my father bought a car, I became the family driver as he didn't have a licence. Most Sundays I took my parents out somewhere for a change of scenery. Sometimes I was allowed to borrow the car and I would go off on my own. Of course, as a young fellow who had just started courting it meant I could boast to my friends, 'I'm taking my girlfriend out for a spin in my car this weekend.'

* * *

It was Easter 1938 when I first saw Lily Mathers. I didn't know it at the time but it was love at first sight. I was coming up to eighteen and like any young man, just wanted to enjoy myself and have a bit of fun. I wasn't looking to get serious with a girl or get married but I felt we had something pretty special early on, Lily and me. I couldn't stop thinking about her and knew that I wanted to be with her; I thought she felt the same although we didn't talk about it. I assumed we had an understanding but things don't always go according to plan.

Most weekends, I used to go out with a group of friends, working fellows like me. We used to put a shilling or two a week into a kitty and when we had enough we would decide what to do. A favourite activity was going up to London by bus or train and catching a pleasure steamer from Tower Pier down to Margate. I remember sailing on the *Golden Eagle*, the *Royal Eagle* and the *Medway Queen*. We had a marvellous time. Funny to think, years later, that many of these boats were requisitioned for war work. While I was being detained at Herr Hitler's pleasure in East Prussia, they were travelling up and down the Thames, sweeping for mines or ferrying evacuees from the East End to the coast; and even into the English Channel to help with the evacuation of Dunkirk.

A return ticket cost about five shillings and we were happy walking round the decks, breathing in the fresh air and enjoying the change of scenery. Day trippers with a bit more money paid extra for a deckchair and sat outside or in an enclosed lounge area. There were kiosks selling food and drink and there was a posh dining saloon with waiters in uniform but I never saw the inside. If we fancied it, we followed some of the other fellows 'to see the engines' as they called it. The bar was situated near the engine room and there was a lot of drinking during the trip and some very merry people by the end. I never got drunk as I only drank lemonade or ginger beer.

After we arrived and docked, we usually had a couple of hours at the seafront, strolling along the Promenade, enjoying an ice cream or paddling in the sea with our trouser bottoms rolled up. Sometimes we went off to Dreamland Amusement Park where there were rides and sideshows but that could get expensive and it was all a bit of rush not to miss the boat home. At other times, back in Barking, when we had less money in the kitty, we went to the cinema and ate fried eggs on toast in a cafe or fish and chips wrapped in newspaper while sitting on the quayside and then larked around town.

One long weekend, which stretched over the whole of Easter, my pals and I went round to a friend's house in King Edward Road. His parents were away so we decided that it would be fun to have a party and stay over. The obvious thing to do was to let all your pals know and make sure that some girls were invited. There were six of us fellows and eight girls, friends from work or church, someone's sister; you know the sort of thing. It was only a small terraced house so it was cosy, you could say, but we moved from room to room, chatting, listening to music on the wind-up gramophone and my pal on the piano accordion and eating and drinking. We didn't make much of a mess but I remember being the one tidying up afterwards, putting things back where they belonged.

I suppose that, by today's standards, our behaviour was pretty tame. The lads didn't go in for binge drinking like now, although some of them used to get a bit merry. A few smoked but I didn't until I became a prisoner of war. I began smoking seriously when the tins of cigarettes started arriving in the Red Cross parcels. I remember receiving a load from a vicar in Surrey who adopted me. I don't know how this came about, whether he drew my name out of a hat for some 'Help a Soldier at the Front' appeal in his parish, I never found out, but he used to send me 400 cigarettes at a time. Of course, I didn't smoke them all. I used some for bartering for extra rations from the German guards.

It was at the house party that I met Lily. As soon as she walked into the front room, I couldn't take my eyes off her. She had lovely brown eyes, beautiful long black hair and a wonderful smile. She was always smiling, even though, I learned later, she didn't have an awful lot to smile about. She was a little shorter than me and was wearing what I call a 'teddy bear' coat, with a furry texture, and a pink scarf. I didn't even notice the others girls.

We started chatting and she seemed to like me. For the whole of that long glorious weekend she hardly left my side except when she went to the kitchen to help make sandwiches with the other girls or they went off to bed upstairs at the end of the evening. I could have walked home each night as it was only fifteen minutes away, but I didn't want to miss seeing as much of Lily as possible. I slept downstairs on cushions on the floor and dreamed of Lily.

What I liked best was walking and I used to go down to Barking Creek where I watched tugs and fishing boats and gulls squabbling overhead. The further I went on, away from the mills, timber yards and gas works, the more desolate it got out near the marshlands. I used to watch herons flying out of reed beds and listen to distant shipping horns. We walked there that weekend. I was happy keeping with Lily, talking and laughing, getting closer to her while the others went ahead or off on their own. Even though I was shy and usually careful about what I said, I felt I could talk to Lily; she was a good listener.

Lily was a seamstress and worked with her sister. In her spare time she loved dancing and she used to sing with a band. She wanted to be a properly trained singer but her mother Ada wouldn't let her. You crossed Ada Mathers at your peril. Lily had to learn a trade. She was very good at dressmaking and made all her own clothes (except the teddy bear coat, of course) and continued to do so all her life. She made all our Brian's clothes when he was growing up. Clever girl.

I have a photo of Lily when she was about 17, here, now, by my side. She is wearing a pretty floral blouse, with three fancy buttons down the front, which she designed and made herself. I have treasured the photo all my life. It was one of my most valued possessions, surviving the labour camps and The Long March home. Lily, always there by my side.

Ada wasn't really to blame for wanting her daughter to have a good trade like dress-making, what she thought was the best for her daughter and the family. We were living in difficult times and every household was counting the pennies. My father, too, thought that earning your keep was more important than following your dreams. Like me, Lily had ambitions which weren't fulfilled although she continued singing with the band until the war broke out. Later, when we were married, I loved hearing her sing around the house, even though I have a tin ear, and I was pleased that our son, Brian, turned out to be musical.

Lily didn't say much about her parents and later on, when I found out more about them, I could understand why she didn't want me to meet them. After that weekend we met regularly, spending our free time together so that I saw less of my pals and more of my girl. I borrowed the family car from time to time when my father let me and I took Lily for a drive around town, or into the country, proud to be seen with my beautiful girl but she never wanted me to drive her home.

I brought Lily to my home a few times, when my parents were up in town and Winnie and Elsie were there. We would sit and talk, have tea and then I would walk her back to Barking Station, get a platform ticket and see her onto the train. It was sad every time I said goodbye to her. If it was hard then, imagine what it was like for me during those five years of captivity without seeing the face of the one I loved and hearing the voice which made my heart miss a beat.

It was a shock, I'll admit, the first time I saw where Lily lived and met her parents. She couldn't really put it off any longer as we had been seeing each other a while and were pretty serious. They lived in Stratford, what I called West Ham, in a rather run-down area in a very small mid-terrace cottage with two bedrooms, a tiny garden at the back and an outside toilet. Lily slept downstairs in the front room so she didn't have a place to call her own.

Alf, Lily's father, was a cooper who repaired barrels for local breweries. He used to get these huge whisky casks brought in on the horse-drawn carts. When they arrived in the yard, he and his mate lifted them off and turned them over onto blocks of wood to drain the dregs into a bucket underneath. You would be surprised how much liquor came out of one of those casks. They would strain the whisky through a lady's stocking set up on a tripod to filter out any impurities, such as dirt and grit which had collected inside. It was then decanted into empty White's lemonade bottles. Alf made himself a special wooden suitcase, lined with cloth, to carry two of these bottles in and out of work each day. No wonder he used to fall asleep drunk every evening and Ada had to help him to bed.

One day he was coming home from work and was so drunk that he fell down the steps in the bus, the suitcase broke and a shard of glass got lodged in his arm. He didn't feel a thing and refused to go to hospital. However, he was taken there in the end to have it seen to and was kept in. I visited him in New Cross Hospital and saw how he was bruised from waist to feet. He still didn't feel a thing and protested 'Fuss 'bout nowt.'

Lily's mother, unfortunately, wasn't much better. Ada wasn't a very nice person and took no nonsense from anyone. She was a cook in a pub and worked long hours for low wages. But that didn't put her off spending every spare penny (and more) on the dogs. She was never happy unless she was having a bet. She even pawned her son Alfred's best suit, the one he wore on Sundays and to go courting. Things were rough at home and I know that one of her sisters married early to get away from the rowing and Lily left home as soon as she could.

Lily and Charlie, Charlie and Lily, whichever way you said it, it was the same: we were a couple. We had been going out together for about 18 months, still enjoying going for walks, to the pictures and the occasional dance but I wasn't keen on that. Two left feet, that's me. Lily would try to get me on the floor but when I resisted, she would go off and have a jitterbug with some other fellow. I didn't mind because I knew I would be hopeless even if I had wanted to have a go. At other times we would just sit at home, snuggling up and enjoying being together. I was saving money and Lily was putting things away for her bottom drawer. No actual plans for marrying had been discussed and, with war looming, our minds were concentrating on what was happening around us and what it all might mean for the future. Would I be called up? Where would I go? What would Lily do? So, the night Lily told me it was all over came as a real shock. What on earth had happened for her to say this? Had she got cold feet or met someone else?

I was at Lily's place one evening, a terraced house she had moved into as a lodger. She had met a woman by chance at the bus stop one evening after work and they had got talking. Lily said she was unhappy at home and mentioned a recent unpleasantness with her mother. This woman offered her a room in her house; her husband was a butler at Buckingham Palace and was rarely at home. Lily was lucky to find somewhere nice to live. I was sitting quietly in the small armchair in her little bedroom as I did three or four times a week. It was cosy with the curtains closed, the lamp on and we could forget the world outside. Lily was very quiet and just sat there on the edge of her bed and I knew something was up.

'Have I done something wrong?' No answer. 'Lily. What is it?' And then those words, spoken so slowly.

'Well, I've been thinking.'

There was a long pause. I could hear people passing in the street, singing and laughing. 'Someone's happy,' I thought. 'Don't say anything,' I said to myself and then out loud, 'Don't say anything else, Lily. Please, don't.'

She sighed and said, 'I'm sorry, Charlie, but I want time to think about us a little bit more.'

She's found somebody else, I knew it. 'Do you want me to go?'

'Do you mind?'

That was it, I had to go then. 'If that's what you want I'll leave.'

I got up slowly, leaned over and kissed her goodbye on the cheek. There was a terrible lump in my throat so I couldn't have spoken even if I had wanted to. I went downstairs, out the front door, shutting it slowly, down the path, shutting the gate slowly too, hoping all the time Lily would come out and call me back. I walked to the end of the road, looking back all the time to check if her light was still on. No light. I walked on to the bus stop, thinking she would run after me. I waited. I could hear the sound of a piano playing in a pub nearby and people laughing, and the far-off rumble of a passing train but no voice calling me back.

My mother was still awake when I got in. Once she had heard the back door go and my footsteps coming upstairs, she could close her eyes and go to sleep. But I couldn't sleep that night thinking about what had happened and wondering what I had done wrong. All alone now. A terrible feeling.

I hadn't seen Lily for weeks, maybe for a couple of months or, should I say, she hadn't seen me. Because during that time, I have to confess something. I followed her and secretly watched where she was going. I missed her but I admit that I also wanted to know if she was seeing somebody else. Once I followed her all the way up Stratford Broadway to the Town Hall where she met some fellow outside and they went in to a dance which was on there. I didn't go inside but she did the same thing the following week. Well, that's it, I thought.

Then one evening she suddenly appeared. I was returning home with my brother-in-law, who was staying with us. It was very dark as we walked from the station as half the street lights were off. Bert saw somebody waiting at the top of the road and as we got nearer I heard my name being called.

'It's Lily,' said Bert, 'you go on, I'll make my own way back,' and he made himself scarce.

'Lily,' I said rushing towards her. 'How long have you been here?'

'I thought I'd missed you.'

I could see she was shivering. 'You're freezing cold,' I said as I touched a hand. 'You've got no gloves.' I took hold of both hands and warmed them with mine. She bent forward and a lock of her hair brushed my cheek and I breathed in the familiar scent of lavender soap. We stood there for a while just feeling the reassuring presence of each other again.

'I'm sorry,' she said at last. 'So sorry, Charlie,' and she put her arms around me and gave me a big hug. Oh, how I had missed that!

'I don't understand,' I said. 'What happened?' Whatever it was it didn't really matter now. 'What was it? What did I do wrong? Tell me and I'll try and put it right.'

She stood back a bit and said, 'You can't dance, Charlie.'

What did she mean, can't dance? Was that what this was all about? 'I'm sorry,' I said. 'I know I'm no good at dancing. It's just that I've got two left feet.' I looked at her and smiled, 'But I can learn, Lily. I'm sure I can, if you want.'

Fortunately for me, Lily saw past my failings and realised she loved me for what I was. I hoped I would make a better partner in marriage than I was on the dance floor. I was lucky, so lucky that she gave me a second chance. I did try to learn to dance years later after we were married. Lily had talked me into taking some dancing lessons but it wasn't any good and I still have two left feet.

As war approached everybody was getting jittery with the news of Hitler's invasion of Poland. So on 3 September, when the inevitable announcement came, it was a kind of relief. We didn't have a radio but word got round quickly about Chamberlain declaring war on Germany. My mother was upset and cried. The last thing she, or anybody else who had lived through the last war, wanted was another one. There was talk about the call up of young men between 20 and 23 years old. That upset my mother and sisters too. It was just a matter of time. My birthday was in May so, as a 20-year-old, I was expecting my papers any day.

When my army call up papers arrived on 18 October telling me where I had to go register, it was a blow when I realised that I wasn't going to join the regiment I had requested. Everybody had to fill in a form sent from the Ministry of Labour and National Service, asking us 'to express your preference' and I wrote down, 'to join the Royal Corps of Signals.'

My school friend, Ronnie, had just joined them and had gone off training not far away. I was looking forward to following him and having a pal around to make it more fun and less frightening.

I imagined that I would be learning Morse Code and how to use a radio transmitter; how to install and repair telephone lines and useful skills like that for the front line boys. I did not want to be in an infantry regiment whose main purpose was sticking bayonets into other men's guts. It was not that I didn't want to do my duty or was going to shirk my responsibility but I just didn't want to have to kill a man, any man, somebody with a wife and children. Why should I kill him?

I honestly believed that there was a choice when I filled in the form. I am in where I want to be, ready to serve my King and Country. I am not afraid of hard work and I want to learn new skills. I will do my job as well as I can and we will all be home by Christmas.

3

All at Sea

There was no choice. I was put in the Queen's Royal Regiment, an infantry regiment, well known for its fighting abilities. It was wrong of them to give you the idea that you had a say in what happened to you. It was one of the first (and there were to be many later on), examples of the helplessness I felt at being in the hands of authority, powerless to decide your own destiny.

I was assigned to the 2nd Battalion, 7th Company which was made up of regulars, volunteer reservists (territorials) and conscripts. A lot of us, especially the conscripts and the young officers, didn't have a clue what to do and we never had any real training. It was the Phoney War; and things hadn't got going properly and we felt as though we were just playing at being soldiers.

I had to report to an address in East Grinstead which turned out to be premises above a furniture store in the High Street. I met another fellow on the train who was going there, and we eventually found it round the back of the building up some stairs. It was musty and damp inside and looked as though the place was used for storage and had just been hastily cleared. There were a dozen or so there already and we joined a queue to register at a desk. Gradually more arrived, until there were about thirty of us by late afternoon. There didn't seem to be anything else to do except sit and wait. One chap said, 'I fancy going out for some cigarettes. Anybody want to come?' A couple put their hands up and were about to leave when we heard the sound of heavy boots coming up the stairs.

The Sergeant Major arrived and stood in the doorway. Nobody moved. He was a ratty little fellow who didn't look as though he was going to take any nonsense from anybody. Straightaway he laid into us, barking commands to line up, stand to attention and don't speak until you're spoken to. He told us in no uncertain terms what he thought of us. He didn't like the look of us, we weren't going to be any good or amount to much, all that sort of caper you get from these people. It didn't sound to me as though we were in for anything good.

It was getting late by then and we were told to bed down there for the night. We slept in our clothes on the floor on what were called 'biscuits', a set of three square canvas cushions laid out to make a bed. Hard as nails they were. Better get used to this, I thought, it was probably a sign of things to come. I don't think I was ever comfortable again at night until I got home to my own bed after the war.

In the morning, after waiting for more recruits to turn up, we were taken by army trucks to the camp barracks to begin our army life. I stuck with the chap I had met on the train and we joined up with another couple of fellows and amused ourselves talking about our families and had a bit of a laugh about the Sergeant Major. I didn't mind being away from home; it was an adventure for us young lads. That night I had no worries about being in a dormitory with a bunch of strangers because I was used to sleeping in the same room with my brothers and with my pals when I was away on holiday.

We were taken to an army store to be kitted out in our new uniforms. Even though mine didn't fit properly and my boots felt tight, I didn't say anything. I would have to put up with it. We went back into town to an army depot and did our first bit of training. We were introduced to various officers and NCOs who told us what their jobs were and how the company worked. We did some running up and down, some marching and tried a bit of basic drill to get us all working together as a unit. I told Lily I had two left feet and this was evident as I tried to keep in step with the other lads.

A few days' later we were all taken down to the army camp at Horsham in Sussex which was to be our base for the rest of our training until our departure for France. We had our medical and 'Protective Inoculations', recorded in my Soldier's Service and Pay Book: 'Nature of vaccine, "T.A.B." Cholera, plague etc.' and I was pronounced 'A' fit for service and therefore able to start the training.

We were out of doors a lot of the time on route marches and exercises. Once we were driven in the back of a lorry at night, dumped in the middle of nowhere and told to find our way back to camp. Marching was hard on the feet all the time and it was very important to break in your boots. You couldn't afford to have blisters and bunions when you eventually went into action.

One of my early brushes with authority occurred when I had been out in town one night and was returning to camp with a friend. We were walking along the High Street, smoking as we went, when we saw an officer coming towards us. We both slowed down and saluted but my pal had the presence of mind to throw away his cigarette. I was still smoking when the officer, a young chap, came right up to me, and slapped me across the face. He just meant to knock the cigarette out of my mouth but he miscalculated. The blow gave me the shock of my life and I finally got the message. You're a man now and you're in the army, Charlie. You're going to have to learn the rules, obey orders and remember your place.

I wouldn't have minded being given a few more orders or at least some guidance. We were ill-prepared for fighting and for what lay ahead. I don't think that I fired more than five rounds of ammunition before I went over to France. We spent a day, I'm sure it was no more than that, on a firing range on Salisbury Plain. Inside one of the huts, the Sergeant demonstrated how to assemble and dismantle a Bren gun and then told us to do it. There were three Brens laid out on tables with thirty of us trying to have a go. The Sergeant got annoyed when we couldn't do it. Some of us barely had time to touch one. Outside on the range, we were given our Lee Enfield rifles – First World War bolt action weapons, and told to lie down on our stomachs and fire at numbered targets allocated to us. I was given Number 6, and the Sergeant tapped my foot when it was my turn to fire. I'm not sure if I hit the target at all because as I fired, the rifle kicked back practically ripping my shoulder off. I was probably firing up in the air for all I knew. I fired a few rounds and then it was time to go back to camp.

And that was it for a while. We carried on doing drills and exercises which I hated. I wasn't a natural soldier, certainly not a killer, so I was very happy when I was selected to join the company transport unit.

It happened one day when we got back from an exercise. The Sergeant Major called us to attention and read out a list of names of men who were to report to his office. A few weeks ago, an officer had asked our platoon for volunteer drivers. 'Write your name and number on a piece of paper and put it on my desk in the office.' There were seven names on the list, including mine, and we were told that we had all got driving jobs. It wasn't like it is now when every youngster learns to drive as soon as they reach seventeen. I was one of the few who had held a licence for nearly four years. As there was a shortage of drivers, I was a good catch. Licences were checked, papers issued and vehicles assigned.

Hand in hand with a shortage of drivers was a shortage of vehicles. The army was using ones which had been hired or commandeered from local civilians – their contribution to The War Effort. Some people were making a lot of money doing business with the army. Horsham housewives found that they were not getting their laundry delivered and butchers in Tunbridge Wells did not have their waste bones collected. So who was it that got one of those lorries? It was me. I got a bone lorry. It was terrible. My uncle was a butcher and every Monday morning one of them came round to collect his waste bones which were collected in sacks and thrown straight into the back of the lorry which continued on its round until it was full. You can guess what that lorry smelt like over time.

Now the chap who had hired my lorry out to the army did his best, or so he thought, to hide the nature of its cargo. He washed it out and cleaned it but, of course, that wasn't enough to get rid of the awful smell. So he decided to paint it inside and smothered it with thick brown paint which only made things worse. There was the smell of old bones and the smell of paint mixed together. I felt sorry for the men I was carting about in it. They were standing up in the back, while I sat in the front cab away from the worst of the stink.

I enjoyed being out on the road, driving around collecting supplies, taking the men out on exercise and all that. I learned how to look after the vehicles and do basic repairs. However, one day I was driving in a convoy going out on manoeuvres in town. Everybody had jobs to do as part of the exercise and I decided to help the lads fill sandbags for a shelter they were constructing. When we got back, I was summoned to the Section Commander's office. What on earth had I done wrong?

I stood to attention while he tore me off a strip for what I had done. 'You left your f------- vehicle!' he said. 'Never leave your f------- vehicle again!' All the regulars swore like troopers. 'That's your f------- job!' My responsibilities were to drive and look after the vehicle. Nothing else. I don't know what he would have said if he had known that a few months' later I abandoned my truck on a road in France and surrendered to the Germans.

You do your best, that's all you can do. In spite of the rollicking I got, I wasn't put off. I was happy to carry on driving and looking after my vehicle, pleased to have this particular responsibility in my unit. However, I didn't know that I was in danger of having it taken away from me and being put right in the line of fire.

A month later, seven of us were called to do some more firearms training but in a different location, inside a tunnel. The rifles we used this time took 0.22 calibre bullets which were smaller and the targets we used were much nearer, about 100yds away. It was a bit like popping a gun at Dreamland Amusement Park in Margate, trying to win a goldfish for your girl. With the smaller bullet there was less kick and it was more accurate firing, and I could see that I was doing quite well. I just thought that it was good fun and a bit of extra training. I didn't know how I had scored until a few days later when five of us were called back to the Commander's office. In trouble again.

We went in one by one and the first thing the chap said was, 'What I'm going to tell you now is not to be repeated outside this room.' Goodness,

I had no idea what was coming next. It was a shock. I had scored highly on the practice range and had been selected to train as a sniper. This is ridiculous, I thought, straightaway. Why would I want to do that? Kill or be killed. I could be up a tree, see a German coming, fire at him, miss him, he turns round, shoots me, and I fall out of the tree either dead or injured. And what about the driving? I had only just got that job and they were going to take it away from me. So I refused – and so did the others. We were lucky that we were able to say no. They were short of snipers but they were also short of drivers, so they would have had to recruit more which would not have been easy.

In early April 1940 we received our orders for departure to France to join the British Expeditionary Force (BEF). We were given a few days' leave and I went home to see Lily and the family. We had a little party and Lily and I managed time on our own, going out on one of our favourite walks. My mind was on all sorts of things and we didn't talk much about the war or about what might happen to us in the future. 'Let's just enjoy being together now,' said Lily, putting her arms around me and holding me tight.

The next morning, as I was about to leave, my mother gave me a gold signet ring. 'Take it, Charlie. It was your grandfather's. I want you to have it.'

I had never bought a ring for myself and had always wanted one. 'I'll always wear it,' I said, putting it on. I never told my mother after the war that I had given it to a German soldier in exchange for half a loaf of bread. When you're starving, you do anything to fill your belly.

I was about to leave my home and my country for the first time. I was pleased and proud to be going out to France, in my brand new Bedford MW truck. Luckily it had arrived in time for me to familiarise myself with driving it and also to practise some basic maintenance work. I didn't know, as I boarded the ship at Southampton that I wouldn't see my family again for five years.

* * *

An apple, an orange, a bar of Fry's chocolate and a pork pie. That's what I collected from the Warrant Officer in charge of stores before I boarded the boat to France on 17 April 1940. A real feast to me. I suppose I remember that clearly now, because food, and finding enough to eat, was an obsession during my years of captivity. There was the luxury of packets of jelly in the Red Cross parcels; the necessity of eating dock leaves and fish heads on The Long March.

All through my life since the war, I have appreciated every crumb of food on my table. A slice of toast is as good to me as a side of beef. I took my rations and went to join the others. 'Let's hope it stays down,' I thought. I didn't want to be seasick. A paddle steamer on the Thames wasn't the same as sailing on a troop ship out into the open sea.

I was excited now that we were leaving England and on our way to be part of this big adventure. The Transport Corps was going ahead of the company to prepare for the rest of the Battalion's arrival and deployment. I stayed on deck with the other men as we waited in Southampton waters before leaving in the early hours of the morning. I ate my food as I watched all the activity on the quayside: so many busy men with so many loads, all shapes and sizes. I talked to the other soldiers who were also in transport and supplies, sent ahead of their units to prepare the ground for them. The sea was calm, the sky inky black and I dozed off, surrounded by the noise of engines and the chatter of men.

When we disembarked at Le Havre our vehicles had already arrived on another boat anchored alongside. As we walked off, our trucks were being lowered in slings onto the quayside. Once they had landed and the slings removed, we had to push the vehicles to the end of the dock and then wait for instructions.

There were seven of us with six trucks and one small tanker which carried all the drinking water for our company. We had been told not to drink any water while in France unless it had been treated. An officer met us in his little two-seater Austin car and directed us to the end of the dock where we filled up with petrol. Then we followed him in convoy out of the port and into the Normandy countryside – remembering to drive on the right-hand side, of course.

It was wonderful being behind the wheel of our new vehicles, following the officer in his motor car out front, taking our time, enjoying the view. Along straight tree-lined roads for miles, through small sleepy villages with shuttered cottages out into the vast countryside. It was so pretty and the roads were empty; it was a pleasure being out there like being on holiday. We stopped by the roadside to make tea and have a smoke. All that clean, fresh air and space, and peace and quiet. Hard to imagine there was a war on. Everything looked normal: washing on lines, men working in fields, cows grazing. War seemed a long away from us.

Our field camp was just outside Abbeville where all the various units had different quarters under canvas. We were in our own little marquee which housed us, some admin people and cooks. When the rest of the Company finally arrived, they would be spread out in a number of different sized tents; the officers having their own separate bell tents. Not that we spent much time there. We were out driving all the time to large field depots to collect supplies of food, water, blankets, equipment, petrol and ammunition to take back and unload at base camp. There was everything you needed to fight a war.

We started work from the moment we arrived and I saw little of local life, especially any French people. Often on my trips the only life I saw were the black and white cows lazing in the shade of trees or gaggles of geese flapping about a farm yard as I roared by. When I arrived at the depot there would be English voices, 'Awright, Chas, me boy, another load for you,' and 'Watch these little beauties over the pot holes' – meaning, take care or you might get yourself blown up by the ammo in the crates. We didn't have anything to do with the French and I didn't see or speak to any locals in the first few weeks. I did eventually though make contact with a Frenchman – literally.

One morning I was driving an officer to a meeting at another camp. I had the empty road to myself and I was bowling along at a fair lick on the left, the wrong side of the road; easy to forget. I had a driving mirror which was specially lengthened and stuck out quite far from the side. I was going up over this bridge approaching a small village and when I came down the other side, there was a French man in his blue dungarees and black cap, cycling very slowly along. As I went passed him my wing mirror hit him on the head and knocked him off his bike. So I slammed on the brakes and was about to reverse to see what damage I had done.

'Don't stop, you clot! Don't you know there's war on?' said the officer. I could see the man in my rear view mirror lying on the road, his bike in the hedge. I could have killed him for all I knew. But orders are orders and I accelerated away, hoping we hadn't been spotted. I was careful to keep on the right side after that.

We carried on half a mile or so and passed some French barracks so I slowed down to get a better look. I was amazed to see a French sentry, rifle propped up against the wall, smoking a cigarette and chatting up two girls. I said, 'You wouldn't get away with that in England, sir, would you?' still thinking of the wallop I had received for having a fag in my mouth from that officer during training. 'They do things differently here, Private.'

So with all this coming and going on various jobs, we weren't doing what I would call regular hours. We went out and came back when the work was finished, whatever the hour. Sometimes we didn't have time to queue up for food at the canteen, so we had to grab food when we could. I found myself doing a lot of eating as I drove along in the truck. I took rations with me such as bars of chocolate, biscuits and tins of stew which could be heated up. I often ate the stew cold, with a spoon straight from the tin as I drove along, trying to keep the truck from landing in a ditch. That's when I thought it would be handy to have someone else to share the driving.

Someone up above must have heard me because it was a couple of weeks after we arrived, that I heard that we were going to be allocated a spare driver. I had just had my twenty-first birthday and I remember that my birthday cards were still under the seat of my truck. I used to read the messages in them over and over during any snatched moments on the road. We had started receiving post from England quite soon after our arrival. I knew that my mother was well and Lily was missing me. We got back in the evening and I was parking my vehicle in my usual spot. I had my head out of the window as I was reversing and could hear all these voices calling out across the field.

'Who's Private so and so?' and 'Who's Private so and so?' I heard my name called out, 'Private Charles Waite.' I got out of my truck, walked across to this fellow and said, 'That's me, Charles Waite. Who wants to know?'

I was disappointed, I have to say. Instead of some fellow like me, the same age, somebody to have a bit of a laugh with, I was looking at this old man. Well, I say old, he was only forty-two, twice my age, but to me he was an old man.

'My name is Moore but they call me "Pony".' He put out his hand.

I never even asked his first name. In the army anyone called Moore was nicknamed 'Pony' so that was his name: 'Pony' Moore.

'Pleased to meet you. I'm Charles but they call me Chas,' and we shook hands.

So Pony and I started working together. I was a bit worried because all these new men and new drivers had been shipped out and I thought my job could be in danger. He was a full corporal, a non-commissioned officer, with two stripes and he was above me so if they wanted to deploy some of us to frontline duties then that would probably be me. I imagined that he would pull rank and start telling me what to do but he didn't at all. He didn't even mention driving and just sat silently in the passenger seat enjoying the view.

One day we came back quite late and very hungry and I was just reversing in to my space, the last one home. Pony had jumped out and gone round the vehicle to check that everything was all right when an officer suddenly appeared, banging on the front of vehicle for me to stop.

'Where's your spare driver?' he asked me, leaning in towards the open window.

'He's here, sir,' indicating with my thumb over my shoulder.

'Call him over.'

'Corporal Moore,' I leaned out and shouted to Pony – I remembered to use his proper name. 'Captain wants a word.' He appeared from behind the vehicle, stubbing out a cigarette and adjusting his cap.

'I want you back on the road pronto. We've got a meeting at HQ. The chateau,' and he mentioned the name. 'You know. You've been going past it practically every day.'

I knew where he meant, the big turreted place surrounded by trees with a long drive going up to it. Two or three other officers appeared and they all climbed in the back as Pony got back in the cab. 'There goes supper,' I said.

I drove back out onto the main road and could hear the men moving about in the back. Pony kept any eye out for familiar landmarks and sign posts and we managed to find the chateau without any wrong turnings. The wheels scrunched on the gravel drive as I edged my way along not wanting to kick up anything which could damage the windscreen. I drove up to the very grand front entrance with its portico and steps leading up to the door and stopped. The men had jumped out by the time Pony had got out and round the back to open the door for them.

The officer came to my window to speak to me. 'All right, private, you don't have to wait. We're coming back by car tomorrow. Off you go back to base.'

Pony got back in and I reversed in the drive and drove back down to the main road. As we were going along, I said to Pony, 'Would you take over for a few minutes so I can have a Maconachie?' You see, I was always hungry and this Maconachie was a brand of beef stew with beans, carrots and potatoes, part of our army rations. I thought it was nice even though most people thought it tasted terrible, especially cold.

Pony turned towards me, 'I'm sorry but I can't.'

I kept my eyes on the road ahead. I didn't know what the problem was and I didn't want to stop so I said, 'OK, get one out and open it for me and I'll eat it as I go along.' So I'm driving along, one hand on the wheel, tin of Maconachie between my knees and eating it with a teaspoon with my free hand.

Later that evening Pony came up to me in our tent and tugging me by the sleeve said, 'Can I have a word, Chas?'

'Yes, of course,' I said, 'Is there anything wrong?' I was wondering if I had put my big feet in something.

'No,' and answering my question with a question Pony said 'What are you?'

I was puzzled. 'I'm a private and I'm a driver,' I said, 'You know that.'

'Where are you from?' he asked.

'From Barking,' I said. Well, he knew where I was from because I had told him when we first met.

'Do you know Charrington's, the brewery?' he said.

I nodded. 'Yes I live about eight miles from there.'

'Well, I worked there as a driver.'

'OK, then, so why wouldn't you drive my truck?'

'No, when I say I was a driver, I mean, I drove a pair of horses. Shire horses, pulling a Charrington's dray.'

You've got to laugh, haven't you? He drove a brewery dray. He hadn't even got a licence and didn't know how to drive my truck or any vehicle, come to that. So there I was with a spare driver who couldn't drive. They called him up and didn't even check what he meant by 'driver' on his application. He should have said something at the time but he didn't. So that's why I landed up doing all the driving. I just hoped that there wouldn't be some emergency such as me being taken ill, or, God help us, injured. Maybe he would have a go. Surely he had watched me enough times changing gear and manoeuvring about to have some idea of what to do.

It was a worrying time. All you could do was carry on with your duties, do your best and be on the alert. When we arrived, we felt as though we were on our holidays but now it was a war zone and this was not going to be any picnic. What were the plans for us? The Germans were rapidly advancing towards the coast and messages from Command HQ made it clear that our company and all the others in the area were there to hold up the Germans, to stand our ground, fight to the last man and the last round.

We were meant to act as the buffer between the enemy and our troops on the beaches of Dunkirk waiting to be evacuated home to safety.

Nobody had bothered to tell me and Pony, Bert and Chalky and all the other drivers how this was going to happen. We may have had our eyes open but we were really driving blind.

4

The Wrong Way

The peaceful French countryside of those early weeks had turned into a noisy and frightening battleground. I heard the sound of aircraft and distant gunfire all the time. I was no longer on the sidelines, out of harm's way. We were right in the thick of it now. Low-flying fighter planes were bad enough, right on top of us as they appeared in the sky only to shoot off again. I stood there trembling even though I recognised them as friendly. We were just tiny specks on the ground to the pilot looking down. How did he know whether we were friend or enemy?

The most frightening sound was that of Stukas, the German dive-bombers, which gave out this dreadful, bloodcurdling siren wail as they dived down and then up again. I was frightened all the time by what was going on around me. Nobody explained what was happening; nobody told you what to do to protect yourself. I was just a driver, trying to look after my vehicle and keep the load I was carrying out of harm's way.

I wouldn't have known what to do if I had come face to face with a German soldier holding a machine gun. I wished then that I had done more training. The sniper course I was offered wouldn't have helped me in these circumstances. The war was a reality now and the fighting was getting closer each day. I was in a constant state of fear. I was doing my best but this proved not be good enough in the end.

We carried on our routine duties of fetching and carrying, going out and coming back, never knowing what might be round the next corner. But you forget all that when you get in the driving seat. You're with your mates, you're out on the road and you're looking forward to your next fag or mug of tea.

Of course, it would have been better to have had some rounds in my rifle the day I was captured. I might have felt braver. Not that I could have returned fire anyway in the face of the German tank unit we met on the road. It happened so fast. And to be honest, I was probably more afraid of my truck being hit – full as it was with cans of petrol. I never usually carried the stuff but on this last trip I had been asked to drive this load of 340 gallons of petrol in tins. They were all packed tight into crates and strapped securely into the back of my truck. I looked at all this fuel in the back as I was loading it, thinking what my father, Alf and Reg wouldn't have done to get hold of a gallon or two for the delivery vans.

The evening of 19 May, we got back into camp and an officer came out and told us not to unload our vehicles but to park and leave them overnight as they were. I thought it was a bit odd until I heard from the other lads later that we were off to Dunkirk in the morning. So our trucks were fully loaded when we left early the next day to do whatever was expected of us, to do our bit in the fight against Germany.

This was the day that sealed my fate for the rest of the war. 'Home by Christmas,' we were told as we left England. But nobody said which Christmas it would be.

* * *

Early morning of 20 May. It was a warm bright day with a light mist just touching the tops of the trees as we drove out from the camp. We could hear a constant low rumbling noise that had gone on all night. I hadn't slept well, listening to the distant sound of fighting and worrying about how close it all was. We didn't know what was going on except that the Germans were closing in on the whole area and we could be caught in the middle. How near I didn't know.

As a member of the transport corps, I knew that my job was to keep the supply chain moving and all I had to do was to follow orders. Nothing very complicated. You didn't have to think for yourself or use your initiative. All it came down to in the end, as my commanding officer said during training – 'Never leave your f------- vehicle!'

It was the driving I loved most, getting out on the road, breezing along with the window down, enjoying the empty roads and open spaces. It was good to have a laugh and a smoke with the fellows in the depot. The last thing I, or anybody else, was thinking about was meeting the enemy face to face and having to defend ourselves. The last time I had fired a gun had been about eight months before on Salisbury Plain. Nobody in charge of my unit there in France had thought of preparing us. Nobody had thought of saying, 'OK, lads, you're out on the road, enemy round the next corner. What are you going to do? You got to be ready for anything. Let's do a bit of target practice. Run through some drills. Check your kit and weapons. Be prepared for any emergency.'

There we were driving all over the French countryside, loading and unloading ammunition for everyone else but nobody had bothered to see if the Lee Enfield rifles we carried were even loaded. I was based at this particular camp and expected to return there at the end of the day. I was dressed as usual in my standard issue uniform, helmet and greatcoat, with a few personal possessions stuffed in the assortment of pockets about me and that was it. That's what I had when I was captured; that's pretty much what I had when I returned five years later.

We were driving in our usual convoy of seven vehicles, water tanker at the rear and me at number 6 with my truck full of petrol tins. I was following the chap in front who was carrying tinned food, including a load of prunes. I remember him joking, 'It's my job to help keep the regulars regular.' The others carried equipment, bedding and, of course, ammunition. As we were about to leave, I saw a young officer rush across towards us and jump in the passenger side of the first truck. Pony Moore was settled in my passenger seat, still half asleep, and I followed the vehicle in front slowly out onto the road, worried about jolting the vehicle too much. Precious cargo – and dangerous too.

We were heading towards Dunkirk on the small country roads through familiar countryside opening up either side. We passed stone farm houses and ramshackle barns dotted about. We came to a halt at a crossroads. There were two cottages, their shutters closed and no sign of life except a couple of chickens scratching around on the verge. I could do with an egg or two, I thought. I only had time to grab a mug of coffee before leaving. Maybe the Sergeant at the depot would let us get a bit of breakfast.

Instead of turning left, as I thought we would, we turned right, the opposite direction back towards Abbeville. Pony wound down the window and poked his head out. 'Lieutenant's waving us on.' You just follow don't you, don't question what you're told to do. It didn't matter to me if we were going another way, I was in no hurry. I assumed the officer knew what he was doing so we dutifully followed.

We left behind the few signs of civilisation there were and came into open countryside with ploughed fields one side and pasture land the other. There were few landmarks except a church spire above a ridge of trees on the horizon. We were driving quite slowly and I kept my eyes on the road, which was higher than the fields, checking for pot holes and making sure the wheels of the truck didn't stray over the edge and down into the gully.

After a few miles we started to slow down, almost coming to a halt again. I wound down my window this time, stuck my head out and shading my eyes, strained to see what was going on up the road ahead. I'm a nosy parker, always wanting to know what's going on and impatient to keep moving. And that's when I saw it – a line of armed vehicles with half a dozen tanks coming towards us down the road.

My first I thought was that this was a bit of luck. They are French, and all we have to do is pull over to one side and let them pass. But then I saw the Black Cross symbols on the sides and I thought that looked like trouble. When I glanced to the right, I saw this dark grey mass of figures like a swarm of ants advancing towards us across the fields. Three or four hundred German soldiers, it must have been. I was scared. I had never even seen a German, let alone hundreds of them armed to the teeth and coming towards me. And that's when I knew we were in a terrible mess.

Everything was wrong. Alone on this road, we had no ammunition, no troops with us. We had no proper firearms, no anti-tank rifles; we had nothing. There was nobody to help us; nobody to tell us what to do. Our officer, who was 2nd Lieutenant and a territorial (and I'm not sure what he knew about anything) was the only armed person with us. He disappeared. What happened to him I don't know; but we were left to face our fate alone.

We tried to get off the road but all that happened was our trucks dropped down the gully and stayed there. The convoy was now caught in the middle of this mass of enemy troops. Terrifying. Pony said, 'Grab your helmet and rifle and get out.' The first and only time I had heard him give an order. I did what he said, put on my steel helmet, grabbed my rifle and, edging the door open, stepped down on to the road.

I was so scared that I dropped my rifle and it went under the truck. No bloody use anyway as I had no ammunition. I knew I couldn't fire back in self defence against this lot even if I had had any ammunition. Hopeless. And then all hell broke out as the Germans opened fire. I threw myself down on my stomach on the side of the road, half under the front of my truck, half in the gully. I lay there absolutely still with my face in the dirt of the road.

I lay there for five or ten minutes, or maybe it was only a matter of seconds. Yet it felt like a lifetime as I blocked out the noise and the fear by thinking of anything else but this horror. I thought of Mum checking the blackout curtains in the shop; Lily sewing buttons on a new blouse; Alfred mending a broken chair at his bench in the shed; Elsie cooking up some nice chops for Joe's tea; and Ronnie joking with his army mates in a bar somewhere safe behind enemy lines. God, what would happen when they read the words 'Killed in action'? All I could hear was the rat-tat-tatting of machine gun fire and the screams. It was a terrible sound, the sound of men yelling out, crying in pain, gasping for breath and dying.

There were Germans firing at us from the other side of the road, lying on top of field ambulances. I turned my head slightly to the side and saw the nearest man to me, only a few feet away. He looked as though he had been cut in half by a machine gun. Shocking sight, all ripped open. Bloody bits of flesh and guts spilling out on the road. He was lying with his head looking towards me, eyes staring blankly and his face was white as though covered in flour. No longer a human being, just some bit of rubbish a butcher had thrown away.

Then it went very quiet. I almost stopped breathing, listening for a sound. Waiting for something to happen. Nothing. And I just lay there, my forehead pressing deeper into the rough stony surface. It was obvious to me that this was our day, our time had come.

So I had it in my mind to get it over and done with quick. Take my helmet off and sit up then they could get a good view of me. They couldn't miss me and I would be shot in the head. That was what I wanted. A nice clean shot through the head. So I lifted my head up and strained an inch or two to get a look. I could see more bodies around and I thought I was the only one left alive. I turned round on my stomach to face the Germans and took my steel helmet off to get it over with and closed my eyes.

A voice called me from somewhere, 'Chas, Chas, are you all right?' It was the Sergeant.

'Yes,' I said, 'I think I'm OK.'

'Get rid of your side arms,' he said, meaning my bayonet. We still had on our overcoats even though it was summer, so I edged myself up slowly onto my knees and then into a squatting position, unbuttoned my coat a bit and undid the webbing which held my bayonet, drew it out and dropped it beside me.

'Now just wait. We'll have to just wait,' he said.

I could see a German officer a couple of hundred feet away, a huge man, flanked by two more gorillas. Anything could happen now, I thought. What will they do to us? The scariest feeling in the world, knowing what these men were capable of and not knowing what they were they going to do. I wished that I had something in my hand, a loaded weapon, preferably. I would have felt better. It would have made me feel like a proper soldier, able to defend myself instead of just being a sitting target.

I was lucky to be still alive though. I felt sorry for the others, particularly those I could hear groaning in pain. God knows what injuries they had and how they would be treated. Then the fear hit me again. What was going to happen next?

At first when I had got out of the truck I thought it would be all right. There's somebody in charge up ahead. We will be OK, they will know what to do. Then I realised I was on my own. I asked myself, 'Why didn't the Germans just blow us all up?' Me, my truck and hundreds of gallons of petrol, it would have all gone off like a bomb and taken us with it. It would have all been over and done with in a second. No fear or no worry. The end. No more. And my last thoughts were for those I was going to leave behind. What would my mother do when she got the news? What would happen to Lily?

The German officer came up the road towards us shouting, '*Hände hoch! Hände hoch*!' – hands up, and 'Up, Tommy, *Hände hoch*!' I was frightened to get up on my own but when I saw the Sergeant move, I grabbed my helmet and stood up. We walked towards the officer with our arms raised high in surrender. Two others of our unit appeared and I was pleased to see one was Pony Moore. As he walked towards them with his hands up, some of the German soldiers started calling out and making gestures. Pony was a short, thickset chap and the Germans were making fun of his appearance shouting '*Komm* Churchill.'

We got up on the road and started walking towards the officer. When he addressed us he spoke quite good English, 'You will proceed,' and pointed. He was a big man, with a square jaw and a ruddy complexion and seemed very excitable. He was drunk. I could smell his breath even from where I was standing.

'Carry on up the road and you will meet my company up there,' he ordered. So we started to walk, three up front, with me and Pony hanging back because he couldn't keep up.

Suddenly there was the crack of a pistol and some bullets whizzed past us. Pony screamed, 'Chas, Chas, help!' I turned and saw the drunken officer waving his pistol around and Pony clutching his hand with blood pouring down his arm. 'Wait, wait! Don't leave me!' I saw what looked like the top half of his thumb hanging off by a piece of skin. I could actually see the bone underneath and the amount of blood was frightening. Poor chap was in awful pain, crying out and clutching his bloody hand.

'I can't leave him,' I said to the Sergeant, so I stopped and turned back to help Pony. 'Hold it up there,' I said, putting his hand in the air, 'I'll get a bandage.' Fortunately, my field dressing pack was where it was meant to be, in my trouser leg pocket. It was easy enough to find but a struggle to open and then to get the dressing out. 'Here, Pony, you'll have to help me,' and he held a corner with his good hand while I ripped the pack open with my teeth and took out the pad and bandage. I did my best to stop the bleeding with the pad and unwound the bandage round and round his thumb.

'It'll be OK,' trying to make light of it. 'We'll have you playing the spoons again.' I used the whole bandage, wrapping it tighter and tighter until I got to the end and tied it off. The blood was seeping through but it was the best I could do. We carried on walking. I don't think the officer intended shooting anyone. He was drunk and waving his gun around, just showing off. Pony happened to be in the way.

We carried on walking for about half a mile while the tanks and troops gradually passed through and on down the road. Now they were going the right way to Dunkirk.

It went quiet again except for the phut, phut of distant gunfire. Pony had his arm on my shoulder and I was guiding him along as he was still in a state of shock. We came to the outskirts of a small village and were ordered to stop, '*Halt!*' We were outside a stone building set back from the road, surrounded by a low wall with iron railings on top. The word *gendarmerie* was carved in the lintel above the door. There were people everywhere, obviously casualties of the fighting and those trying to help. Stretcher bearers with wounded soldiers, men sitting and lying on the ground, people coming and going. Noise and confusion.

The village police station was being used as a temporary hospital in a desperate attempt to cope with the appalling and unexpected number of casualties. We were ordered, '*Hinsetzen!*' – sit, and '*Stehen bleiben*' – stay, as the officer pointed to the wall outside. I helped Pony to sit down and we sat with our backs to the wall listening and watching what was going on. Complete chaos.

Every few seconds we heard a terrible scream or someone yelling. Another German officer came towards us and beckoned us to stand. He spoke good English too and told us that anybody who was injured, and he pointed at Pony, was to go inside where they would be seen to and those who weren't, meaning us, would be directed to 'Lend assistance' as he put it.

I thought that sounded better than sitting about worrying about what was going to happen next. If we could help some of these poor devils who were in terrible trouble that was a good thing: fetching water, carrying a stretcher or comforting a soldier. At least we would be out of the direct line of fire.

'Schnell' – hurry up. We were pushed towards the front door. '*Gehen Sie nach innen,* ' – go in, which we did. Pony followed me in and he was taken away by someone straightaway and I never saw him again. It was dark as I came in from the bright sunlight, and the place felt cold and damp. It was packed with people: men everywhere, standing, squatting, lying on stretchers and on the bare floor. Others were squeezing past bringing in more men and taking others out, presumably ones who had died from the look of them. What a noise! All the languages of the world, it seemed, being spoken but words of pain and suffering are universal. The heat from all the bodies crammed in together was overwhelming.

There was that awful smell of dead meat and stale blood reminding me of Uncle Joe's butcher's shop. I was used to seeing cuts of meat on a marble slab and half carcasses hanging up on metal hooks. The smell of bones and animal waste, which had been hanging around a while, was familiar to me, wafting as it did into our kitchen from next door. But this was something else.

As I walked further inside, I could hear my army boots clomping on the wooden floor boards. There were only four or five small rooms and they were crammed full of men. Some were still like corpses, others screaming and shouting and writhing about. I couldn't hear the sound of my feet and felt the soles of my boots sticking on the floor. I looked down to see trails of fresh and congealed blood everywhere. Wounded men were crying out in pain as they waited to be treated. Those who were uninjured were trying to help, holding bloody bandages and field dressings which couldn't cope with the terrible injuries some of the men had suffered. There were fellows operating in every space and corner, on tables and on the ground where the wounded lay. Whether they were doctors or medical orderlies, I don't know, but they were doing their best to help those most in need.

I was shocked. This shouldn't be happening. This was just an ordinary, everyday place where the local French bobby drank his coffee in the morning and locked up a few drunks or petty criminals overnight. We had no time to take it all in as we were thrown in at the deep end. We stood to attention and waited instructions. In a mixture of English, French and German, men, some recently captured too, in blood-stained uniforms started shouting out commands: 'Hurry up, hold this one down,' and 'You over there, take that man's head,' and 'Don't move an inch or he'll die.' Who was enemy and who ally, didn't matter now. We were all the same there.

I thought of taking off my army greatcoat to put it somewhere safe from this bloody mess. It was a precious possession, even though I had cursed it in this hot summer weather. But there was no time to worry about that sort of thing. Just as well that I didn't remove it as I would never have seen it again.

I certainly needed my coat later on when we were on the move again and started the first march of our captivity. That same coat saw me through the war and was a life-saver on the second march, which took me home half way across Europe.

I had to do it. Just get on with it. Holding down these fellows while they were operated on, just there on a kitchen table, without anaesthetic and with only the most basic surgical instruments. One of us stood at the head and one at the feet. There was no time to be squeamish. Steel yourself and get on with it. I tried not to look at the doctor as his knife cut into the skin and the blood spurted out. Or at them when they were struggling to resuscitate somebody whose heart had finally given up.

I thought of my dear pet dog, Peter, holding him while he had his fits and whispering words of comfort. So I did the same to these bloody strangers. I held them tight and told them, 'Everything is going to be OK.' It was a losing battle in some cases. Better to have tried, I suppose, than not. And if a chap passed away in my arms, I held him for a moment and said a little prayer. Then he was carted off somewhere and another poor soul took his place in the make-shift operating room.

You can't prepare yourself for something like this. I had never seen a dead person in my life. I got upset when Peter died and I had to bury him, so imagine how I felt now. It was bad enough seeing your friends dead or dying on the road side and poor Pony in such pain, with his thumb hanging off. Here I was, a twenty-one-year-old greengrocer's assistant, four weeks into the war without any proper training, facing this dreadful ordeal.

If somebody had told me beforehand: 'Private Waite, your duties are to assist army doctors in their operations on the battlefield,' I would have said, 'Not bloody likely. Find somebody else.' Even now after all this time it upsets me to think about it, those poor men, the pain they were in and the dreadful conditions the doctors worked in, trying to save lives. Bullets and shrapnel were being taken out of legs, arms and chests – wherever the damage had been done.

There were different nationalities including French and Senegalese, probably about a hundred men there. Some were walking-wounded and others had been brought in from where the attacks had been. I think we were only there about three or four hours, that's all, but it felt like weeks. I grew up that day. So much had happened to us since we had taken the wrong road to Dunkirk. Things went quiet all of sudden. Perhaps they had run out of patients but someone came in and ordered us out. We were on the move again and I followed the others outside, back into the midday sun.

We joined another group of prisoners with their guards and we marched to the edge of town just outside Abbeville to a large barracks, which turned out to be a French prison. We were all mixed up and then shoved in five or six to a cell where we slept on straw and dirt on the floor that night. I wasn't one of the lucky ones who got a drink of water and a crust of bread in the morning. This was good preparation for the hardship and starvation which followed. I was separated finally from my company and anybody I knew. I was truly alone.

A week later, my parents received a telegram saying that their son, Private Charles Henry Waite, of the 2/7th Queen's Royal Regiment was 'Missing in Action'.

5

Like Cattle

Details of some events are as clear today as ever, sharpened by the retelling; others not as precise as time has passed. But impressions of particular experiences are so real that I am close to tears as I write this. Fear, anger, humiliation and sadness fill my heart, and even the distance of seventy years does not really lessen these feelings. Whatever we were as young men, as newly recruited soldiers, we did not deserve what happened to us.

So this was what war was like. Bloody chaos. No one was properly prepared for it on either side it seemed to me. A terrible mess of casualties, which no one knew how to cope with; hundreds of prisoners and nowhere to put them. Who knew or even cared about us? I was afraid all the time of what the Germans were going to do. Having no control over anything in your life is very frightening. You have got used to a routine in the army, following orders and instructions from officers, knowing what your job is and working towards the same goals: fighting Hitler and bringing peace to Europe.

The men I met along the way over the next few weeks told stories about mistakes and accidents, bungled attacks, poor defences and dead and injured left where they had fallen. I heard about a massacre not far away where hand grenades were thrown by German soldiers into a barn full of British soldiers who had surrendered and been locked in for the night. I was afraid something like that would happen to us.

My war was over as far as I could see. I was completely in the hands of the enemy. As long as I could keep going for the next few months (and I still believed it would be over by Christmas) stay out of danger, cope with whatever lay ahead then I would get back home safely. But you don't know what lies ahead do you. And you don't know what inner resources you have to draw upon to survive because you have never really been tested.

I know that somehow I got from Abbeville to Trier, a distance of over 350km. I marched to that dreadful city, the place where thousands of prisoners were being processed to be sent on to camps all across Germany and Poland. They had to wait for transport, which for many, including me, meant by train in a cattle truck. But to be honest, my memories of the 1940 march have merged with those of the second march in 1945 – the much longer and much worse one. Not surprising that I forget the details of that summer of 1940. It was only a taste of what was to come during that second march: walking all day with little food or water; sleeping in the open air or finding shelter in barns or under hedges; and abused by German guards. It was hot weather and I was still wearing my greatcoat but I was in good physical shape. But in 1945, we had the additional challenges of one of the coldest winters on record that January, of having suffered years of misery, fear, exhaustion and starvation and of watching fellow men die and helping to bury them by the roadside. Those are things you never forget.

So I know I walked with other prisoners, the group growing as more and more men joined us along the route. We were accompanied by armed German guards, as we made our way across France and Belgium to the Luxembourg border with Germany. I remember that as we went through villages, French women were putting buckets of water out for us at the side of the road and as fast as they did that, the Germans guards kicked them over. The cruelty of that stuck with me, and I remember thinking that this was only the start of something terrible.

We arrived at the outskirts of Trier where there were twenty or thirty fellows all dressed in black, lining the road. They were holding sticks and shouting, 'Sons of English bitches!' over and over again. They started beating the legs of the weakest ones, who could hardly stand anyway, as we passed. Could things get any worse?

I couldn't have imagined the horror that awaited us on the next leg of our journey, travelling a further 1000km deeper into unknown territory, somewhere far over in the East.

When we eventually reached the railway station, we were not alone. I saw hundreds of British soldiers, those recently captured in Belgium, who had just arrived from holding camps. They were grouped on the platforms and down on the tracks while armed guards patrolled. There was an engine being shunted along a track until it made contact and was attached to a row of cattle trucks standing in the sidings.

Suddenly there was a terrific banging sound as guards marched along the tracks unbolting and sliding back the doors of the trucks which gaped open like monstrous mouths, ready to swallow us up. The guards were in a hurry to get the job done, to get rid of all these unwanted, useless prisoners. They started rounding up groups, pushing them at gun point towards the doors like livestock going to market, perhaps to be slaughtered. I could see that when one truck was full they slammed and bolted the doors and then moved on to the next empty one. We were helpless to do anything except wait our turn.

We were marched down to the tracks and herded towards the waiting men. Guards tried to line us up, but we were all in a heap, pushing forward, not because we were keen to board the train but the sheer pressure of the numbers and the panic got us in a mess. A sudden noise of gunshot. One of the guards fired in the air, thank heavens, only as a warning, and everyone stopped dead where they were. When it was our turn we were all pushing forward so we had to scramble up and into one of these trucks. There was a sergeant with us who had torn his stripes off; you could see where they had been. He tapped each of us on the head, almost as if he was blessing us as he counted us in: fifty-seven men reduced to the status of animals.

Inside it was as bad as you imagined. There was dirty straw on the floor and a dreadful smell of excrement and urine, left behind by recently transported livestock or another human cargo. Before the doors were shut some pails of water were put in and someone threw in some loaves of bread (which turned out to be stale already when they were shared out) and a couple of round cheeses. Luckily some of the fellows still had their army jack knives, which had escaped the guards' previous searches.

We were packed in tightly and you had to stand or you could just about sit down with your knees drawn up to your chest. When the guards shut the doors, most of the light disappeared and we were left with what came through gaps in the wooden slats of the sides. When night fell it was pitch black. We had no idea where we were going or how long we would be in there. It was a shocking experience. Some were wearing their greatcoats like me, others just their basic uniform but you can imagine how hot it got with us all crammed together with no proper ventilation. Add to that, the stink of unwashed bodies and our filthy, shitty, lice-infested uniforms; it was unbearable but I had to bear it. To survive and not give in was the only way to beat the bastard Germans.

We were all severely dehydrated and some of the weaker ones were suffering from heatstroke. Nothing you could do. You couldn't move to give them more space – there was none. The train stopped a couple of times, just long enough for guards to open the doors, refill the pails and put them back in. I never got a drink. Most of the water slopped out of the pails anyway, as our truck bumped and lurched along at speed or it was drunk by those nearest to the pails. Every man for himself, I was learning.

It was a rough time, even for the fittest men and many were in a sorry state, already ill with a fever and the runs from their weeks of marching across France and Belgium. Obviously there was no toilet, and no room to move to a corner out of the way in order to do your business. The soldiers who still had their steel helmets ripped out the linings and padding from inside and used them as chamber pots, passing them over for somebody to use and then passing them back with their contents over to somebody on the side. They tried to get rid of what they could through cracks or holes in the floor or emptied them in a corner out of the way. Some men couldn't get a helmet in time and had to shit in their pants where they stood.

God knows how I escaped catching dysentery. Perhaps it was just as well that I didn't drink any of the water or eat the bread or cheese which had been passed around by hands which had been holding helmets of shit and piss. When we arrived at the field camp I remember seeing hundreds of discarded steel helmets all over the ground. Nobody could wear their helmet again, even if they had wanted to, with no padded lining.

How could one human being treat another in this way? I was brought up to believe 'Do no harm' and 'Do as you would be done by.' How could they do this to us? We cursed Hitler, the German people, the war, even the British Army for sending us here. Some men were so exhausted or demoralised they never said a word the whole journey. Others talked a bit about what had happened to them, but not for long. Afraid. We were all terribly afraid and talking made things worse. Nobody had any words of comfort. How could they? 'It'll be all right.' We couldn't say that, not after what we had experienced since being captured. Silence was our refuge.

It was impossible to sleep in more than short bursts what with the noise of the wheels on the track, the constant battering we got as we bumped against the sides and each other, and the cramps in your joints. All I did was catnap, afraid to go into a deeper sleep, I think, in case I didn't wake up. The feeling of suffocation was immense, what with being locked inside this hellish crate, pressed up against other men's stinking bodies, you could imagine yourself just drifting into unconsciousness and never waking up again. I managed to survive the eternity of that train journey towards my long sentence of imprisonment, watching the track under my feet, through the cracks in the floor as the miles sped by.

It seemed never-ending. Sometimes we slowed down for a passing train and those at the side tried to peep through the gaps to see where we were. Then we moved off slowly again and speeded up and then off again. Mile after mile after mile, speeding on and on, as we went further into Germany, across Poland out towards the East. How much longer? How much further? On we rattled and banged about in these brutish conditions, getting weaker and weaker and more disheartened.

On the third morning, the train came to a juddering halt. Was this it? Had we arrived? There was a long silence and nobody dared speak. What was going on outside? What was going to happen next?

Then all hell broke loose. A tremendous noise of banging and clattering, men shouting, boots thumping, and doors smashing back. We were fourth or fifth down and our door was unbolted, pushed back and sunlight streamed in. We shaded our eyes and you could see what a sorry state we were all in. Nobody wanted to catch anybody else's eye because what you saw was just a reflection of yourself, reminding you how low you had fallen. Ashamed of what was happening to us.

Dirty and dishevelled, hunched in pain from the confinement and illness, some managed to stagger out of the door and get down onto the track. Others just fell out, broken men, and didn't get up again. I had difficulty getting out, practically crawling along the truck floor after the others to get to the door. My knees and legs nearly buckled under me as I touched the ground with my feet.

Free at last! Fresh air and space to move about. Then you saw where you had ended up after all that travelling – another dirty railway station siding in some scrubby countryside in the middle of a country you'd never heard of, the only signs you could make out could have been in Arabic for all you knew. Where in God's name were we?

East Prussia, heading for Stalag 20A at Thorn (now Torun, Poland), which was the administrative centre for processing prisoners into the system. According to my International Red Cross records, I arrived there on 10 June and was registered and issued with my metal identity dog tag on which my POW no: 10511 was stamped. I signed my admission card on 26 June 1940 but I have no recollection of staying there. At some stage I was sent on to Stalag 20B at Marienburg (now Malork, Poland) near the Baltic coast which was where I was registered and then sent out to labour camps where I stayed until 23 January 1945.

It was impossible to know exactly where you were most of the time. Always hungry and tired, always afraid and in unfamiliar surroundings, it's not surprising that we didn't know what was going on. You joined a queue here, waited in a line there. You only thought about how to get through the day and survive the night. You lived in the present moment. I met so many different men, fellow prisoners, coming and going that I lost any sense of time or place.

How many prisoners of war were there? Where were they all staying? We were moved around all the time, from camp to camp, and very few men found themselves with people from their own regiments, always being divided and separated, divided again, and sent to various camps and forts, miles from the main Stalag. I don't know if it was a deliberate act and a way of controlling us or just due to the sheer volume of men. All I know is that we were always marching somewhere and always for long distances.

We arrived at an enormous field camp where thousands of men were spread over the area. There were many different nationalities but they all looked in the same poor condition – dirty and half-starved. They were standing, sitting and lying down wherever there was space. There were some small tents pitched on the site and some large marquees which served as kitchen and canteen and quarters for the officers. We queued to have our papers checked and stamped and told to join a line to get our first bit of food. Queuing is what prisoners did most of their waking time.

We were told to stay there and get our soup because if we moved we would lose our place and wouldn't get anything. We had to wait patiently for our turn, hoping that the food wouldn't run out before we got there. The food turned out to be soup which was at least hot and wet and helped take the edge off our raging hunger. I think it was then that my stomach started to learn not to expect much, certainly not ever to be full again; to be satisfied with whatever it was given to keep starvation at bay. Mostly soup as it turned out.

I can't be sure how long we stayed there, a couple of nights, maybe, sleeping on the ground, getting a wash with a tin mug full of water we were allowed from a standpipe; and getting more soup. One time when

I came out of the kitchen tent, an armed guard indicated with his rifle that he wanted us to move elsewhere, directing us towards another queue. Another guard pointed at his head and mimed a pair of scissors with two fingers, shouting at us, '*Haare schneiden*,' – hair cut. Now I didn't fancy having my hair cut, or to be more precise, head shaved (I had seen what the other men looked like) so I decided to take a little stroll around instead and see what was going on.

I noticed a group of men gathered across the other side of the field and could see a horse and cart. Now I'm a nosy so-and-so and like to know what's going on and I decided to go over. I thought it was better to be doing something than just standing around waiting for goodness knows what to happen next. I walked past the end of the barber's tent and out across the open field. The grass was uneven and worn in patches and I had to watch my step, so I was busy looking at my feet.

Suddenly I felt somebody grab my shoulder from behind. I jerked to a stop and spun round to come face to face with a German officer. '*Du,*' – you, '*arbeiten*' – work. He pushed me forwards and I stumbled on towards the other men who were about to get in the back of this vehicle. It was a battered old farm cart drawn by a tired-looking horse, with an equally tired-looking civilian driver holding the reins. The officer counted us on. '*Vierzehn, ja*' – fourteen, yes. '*Das ist gut*' – that's good. There were two armed guards with us, one up front and the other at the back with us squeezed in together. And off we went, bumping along over the uneven ground until we reached an exit out of the wire-fenced compound where a guard waved us through and out.

You can't plan these things, can you? You don't know what fate has in store. Didn't have any choice, anyway – that's the way it goes. Curiosity got the better of me. I was going to say I was lucky to join these thirteen other men but you might say it was out of the frying pan into the fire. I have thought about this a lot lately, and still wonder what would have happened if I had stayed and had my hair shaved off. Where would I have gone? Whilst it was no picnic what happened next, I do think I was saved from something far worse.

* * *

The countryside we drove through didn't look that different from Northern France except for the sheer scale of it: immense stretches of open empty land with town and hamlets much further apart. There were fields lying fallow, others planted with row upon row of crops as far as the eye could see, broken up by the occasional wooded area of conifers and derelict farm buildings. We were driving in a region known as Kreis Rosenberg and we passed near a town called Freystadt.

We finally arrived at a rundown farmhouse. A rough-looking man came out and talked to the driver who hitched the reins to a post and got down, followed by the two guards. In a mixture of German and Polish from the sound of it, the guards exchanged words with the farmer who then came over to take a look at us. He returned to the guards and as he talked started pointing to various buildings around. We got down from the cart and, with a rifle nudging us in the back, walked towards the farmhouse.

I thought for a moment that we were going inside to meet the farmer's wife and have a drink, perhaps. Instead the farmer took us round the back to a large wooden building and pointed to the door at one end. The guard shouted, '*Hinein*,' – go inside. Oh God what on earth was going on? '*Hier schlafen*,' – sleep here, said the farmer. It was a cowshed. Welcome to our new home. From cattle truck to cattle shed.

It was dark and very smelly inside. Much worse than the stables behind Grandma's house which I used to clean out for my brothers, Alf and Reg. The shed was divided in two by a wall which came to about six inches from the roof. There was a herd of twenty-five to thirty cows one end and fourteen men at the other. Wooden boards had been put down on the floor, which was better than the cobbles the animals had next door. You could hear their hooves all the time as they moved about. The straw in their stalls didn't seem to dampen the sound much. There were seven bunk beds crammed in, barely room to move between them. There were a few thick glass bricks high up but hardly any light came through the dirt and grime on them.

We found out later how dark it really was and stifling too, when the double doors were shut and the bar put across outside to lock us in at night. Middle of summer, of course, and no ventilation and the cows next door giving off a terrific heat as well as. So one night, when everybody was asleep, we knocked out a couple of the glass bricks to get in some fresh air. Boy, did you need fresh air with that lot next door.

I managed to get a top bunk which was lucky as I knew about rats on farms and didn't want to give any of those big buggers a chance to nibble my toes as my feet hung over the end of my bed. Fortunately the rats stayed away preferring the livestock next door. If you opened the doors to the cowshed and clapped your hands, dozens of rats, some the size of a cat, mothers and little babies, shot out from under the straw from every corner. The disadvantage of being on the top was that you were nearer the roof and could see the mice running along the gap at the top of the wall. Mice didn't bother me.

Although the stench from the cows was horrible, we were grateful later on in winter for the heat generated by the animals next door. To be honest you were so exhausted all the time that nothing much disturbed you once your head hit the straw mattress. There was a wood burning stove which was out of action most of the time we were there, so it was no use for heating the shed. We didn't have any fuel anyway except what we could find and bring back in dry weather.

We managed, very occasionally, to have a hot (well, warm) bath, taking water from the outside tap in a bucket and heating it up on the stove if we'd managed to get it going. The farmer's wife had left us an old tin bath which was hanging on a nail outside. It was a real palaver but worth it, even for a scoop or two of dirty, grey lukewarm water over you. I used to share the water with Tommy Harrington, one of the fellows I made friends with, and we scrubbed each other's backs. Goodness, what dirt that came off us! It wasn't surprising that we got filthy dirty, considering where we were sent to work. I suppose the sound of blasting in the distance should have given us a clue as to what was going on nearby and why we'd been sent there.

As soon as we had seen our quarters, we were led out of the farm and marched about 5km away. The next shock after our sleeping quarters was that we were not going to work on the farm as we thought but going to a stone quarry. We were sent to work immediately. No training was needed, no special equipment just a hammer and a pair of strong hands for breaking up the rocks.

Once the blasters had done their job with the dynamite on the rock face, we were called in to break up the boulders into pieces and load the stones into railway trucks, which then went off to be used in construction work and repairing roads and railways. We worked in pairs smashing the rocks up with 7lb sledgehammers and then when we had a load, we scooped them up into these large, heavy, wooden boxes. They had handles at each end so we had to carry them together down a slope to the railway trucks which were waiting on the tracks below.

Each truck was numbered with a white card which had 10T, 15T, 20T or whatever tonnage it was, printed on it, and we had to tip the stones out in to the trucks. We kept on doing this for hours on end, every muscle hurting, our hands cracked and bleeding – no shovels or gloves for this work. Was this what I was going to be doing for the rest of the war, however long that might be? Twelve hours a day, seven days a week. Was this better than being shot in the head? Over and done with quickly. No more fear, pain, suffering or humiliation like this.

Every day was much the same: up at 6am exhausted, wash under the tap, coffee, walk to quarry, work, lunch, more work until 6 or 7pm, walk back, supper, go to bed exhausted. The guards changed about four times during the day and we had about half an hour's break for lunch. We were lucky if we got a piece of bread as normally it was just a serving of soup brought up by cart in a milk churn from the farm. It was always rubbish anyway.

In the evening we got our bread, which was supplied by the Germans, and a bit of margarine or sometimes, instead, a piece of *leberwurst*, liver sausage. We got a little bit more of that because I think it was cheap as the locals liked this sort of sausage. Every little bit extra helped to fill us up but, of course, it was never enough. We knew what the rations should have been: 500gms of bread and piece of margarine about the size of a match box, but we never had that.

We only got to hear about other POWs and how they were being treated later on when we moved about more and mixed with chaps from other camps further away. At least we weren't down the mines which were really dangerous places to be. Filthy air, gas explosions and tunnel collapses. We were stuck out here in the middle of nowhere with no news coming our way and we had no idea what was happening in the war. All we knew was our own little world; a world of slavery to our German masters. We were doing their dirty work and helping them instead of helping our own men and our own country. That was a dreadful feeling. We couldn't take pride in anything we were doing. We were the lowest of the low.

We talked a lot about this among ourselves and someone came up with the idea of a bit of sabotage. To do something to make us feel less like victims. Something which would hinder the work but not get us into trouble. Nothing worth getting shot for. Most of the time we only had a couple of guards hanging around while we were working and they weren't watching us all the time. They got bored and went off for a smoke or eat the bread and cheese they had brought with them. They were meant to supervise what we did and check the loading of the trucks but they didn't.

We did the same work every day, breaking up endless rocks and shifting them to the trucks, so we couldn't do anything obvious like stopping work or slowing down even. There were targets to meet for the work: so many trucks filled per day and then taken off down the line to be replaced by another lot to fill. Our great plan for a bit of sabotage was to ignore the weight limits on the trucks and start loading them with more or less the same amount of stones up to the top. While the guards weren't looking we continued filling the trucks with as many stones as we could beyond the markers on the side, ignoring the weight restrictions. That felt good. It gave you back a bit of control and a feeling of power. The trucks would then go off down the line. We watched them disappearing, wondering what would happen next, if anything.

A few weeks' later the *Bahnpolizei* – Railway Police, turned up at our farm to check us out. It was another sunny day, hot already in the early morning and we were all in the yard at the back, some washing under the tap, others hanging around waiting their turn or sitting on a wall drinking the black *ersatz* coffee brought out to us by the farmer – his attempt at providing us with breakfast. I always wondered if he was paid for putting us up or whether he had been told to do it. You didn't refuse orders like that. I think whole families were threatened with deportation if they didn't obey the German authorities. We hadn't heard a vehicle arrive but two men suddenly appeared, marching purposefully towards us in their crisp uniform, shiny boots and eagle and swastika insignia on their braided caps. This looked serious.

They lined us up and took a roll call. One policeman spoke quite good English and he announced that one of their trains carrying stones from the quarry had derailed. One of the axles had buckled under the weight of some overloaded trucks. He said, 'Incorrect weight' and that the overloading of these was 'a deliberate act of sabotage,' and there would be serious consequences for all of us. What was he going to do? Arrest us all and put us in prison? Stop us breaking up rocks? Wasn't this punishment enough? He said that this was to stop immediately. He couldn't prove anything, luckily.

Maybe we were too valuable as workers to get rid of us or waste good manpower by locking us up. I like to think that we did our bit to delay some of the construction work. We heard no more about it and it looked as though we had got away with it but we had understood the message.

6

Potatoes

We carried on working there until Christmas in rain and shine, wind and snow. If it was sunny we worked without protection and suffered dehydration. If it rained we got wet and our clothes never dried out properly and we caught colds. If it snowed we had to dig our way out first before we even got there and nearly collapsed from exhaustion. Some men fell ill or got injured and were sent back to the camp to be replaced by more prisoners. I didn't know the meaning of hard work until I went to that quarry.

Hard physical labour is exhausting and soul-destroying but somehow you survive; it toughens you up. You didn't complain, you just got on with it. So I suppose I was lucky that I didn't go under. A 5ft 7¼", 130 lbs (according to my army records) greengrocer's assistant from Barking, not big and burly or tough, I had never lifted anything heavier than a sack of potatoes. But here I was still in one piece, having no choice but to carry on, to face whatever my captors had in store for me. To keep on going, for myself and for those left behind at home.

I suppose I was lucky not to be sent to another quarry to break up more bloody boulders or to be sent down the mines to be killed by an explosion or tunnel collapse. Our fate was completely in the hands of our enemies. The longer we were imprisoned and got further into the war, we learned more about the cruelty of the Germans and, of course, I was to witness myself some of the atrocities inflicted on other human beings.

I remained at the next camp I was sent to for the rest of the war, along with the four friends I made. Fortunately I've always got on with people and there's something about me that they like. So when I met Laurie, Sid, Hebby and Jimmy we all got on straightaway. We gradually formed a friendship which lasted long after the war.

If you have one good friend you are lucky but to have four is a miracle. How truly blessed to be surrounded by people who care about you, look out for you and stick by you. You get strength from being with people like that. I felt the same, of course. You give as much as you take with true friends. Up until then I had only had one real friend, Tommy Harrington, but that didn't last. He went off to another camp. I remember that he carried a picture of his sweetheart which he was always showing us. She was a real cracker, looked like a film star. I don't think he had any family to speak of so I gave him my sister's address before he left and when I next wrote to Winnie I asked her to keep in touch with him. Winnie wrote regularly and sent him cigarettes. I've got some copies of the letters he sent to my sister.

The strangest thing is that I met him again briefly on The Long March in 1945. Fantastic coincidence, out on the road, among the thousands of people there were on the move across Germany.

You get strength from having friends and together in a group you are better than being on your own. I would have gone mad I think without my pals. Five of us together felt like a family again; reminded me of my brothers and what I was missing. We stayed together for the next 4½ years and I know we helped each other to survive throughout those war years.

One morning at roll call, the *Unteroffizier* – under officer, announced that we were leaving and moving to another camp. We were told to pack and be ready outside as soon as possible. I was pleased not be going out to break up more bloody boulders for twelve hours and glad to see the back of the cowshed. On the other hand, we didn't know where we were going next or what the Germans had lined up for us. We got onto the carts accompanied by some of the guards and set off in the direction of

Freystadt. Just outside the town we stopped at a place which looked like an abandoned school, got off and were split into two groups. I went off with one lot of seven, marching a few more kilometres to another spot where I joined another larger group waiting with some guards.

There were now forty-five of us and we all marched off out into the countryside to a farm in the middle of this remote area. Our new camp was housed in a former farmhouse which had presumably been owned by a local German family. It was now run by the German authorities and we were the new labour force, to be put to work on the land to produce food for the Fatherland. They had built an extension onto the main building for the *Unteroffizieren* and about thirty guards who changed regularly. The whole place was surrounded by two lots of chicken wire fencing with a gap between and rolls of barbed wire along the top. There were two sets of gates, which were locked at night.

Our accommodation was in a large farmhouse which had about seven rooms although we were only allowed to use a few. We slept in dormitories on the ground floor, with ten to a room in double bunk beds. We had the use of a room at the back which had a wood burning stove for cooking and a copper for heating water for washing and laundry. What luxury! And toilets, or latrines I should say, which were in a wooden outhouse. A trench had been dug in the earth floor and you stood or squatted over it

Map showing Langenau and Freystadt in Kreis Rosenberg region, East Prussia. From Bildarchiv-Ostpreussen.de.

to do your business and when you finished you shovelled over some lime from a bucket kept at the side. We could only use them during daylight hours.

We were mainly employed on farm work, providing agricultural labour for anything and everything that needed doing to get food to the German nation. We went out on work detachments locally and further afield, depending on what the work was. Day in, day out, month in, month out, the seasons came and went and the years passed in this vast, desolate wilderness of East Prussia. Fields were ploughed and sown; crops planted and harvested. Fences were mended and roads cleared. Coal unloaded and timber cut down. We turned our hands to whatever was needed. No matter the weather, we were out working away with our bare hands and a few basic farm tools. Muscle power and stamina were what was needed; not brains.

I was happy being out in the fresh air. Perhaps, 'happy' is too strong a word. Rather say 'pleased' because you couldn't really be happy imprisoned where we were in those conditions. It was wonderful receiving a letter from home, a parcel of clothes, extra rations and cigarettes in a Red Cross parcel. It was a miracle and cheered us up but I never felt happy. I was grateful that I wasn't down a coal mine or lying sick or injured somewhere. But not happy.

In spite of the hard physical work, I thought I was freer and healthier than if I had been stuck indoors at some of the other places. Doing nothing but look at four walls of a hut with the occasional bit of exercise round the yard to break up the monotony. Keeping busy during the day helped to distract my mind from thinking about what was going on around me and what the future might bring; but at night dark thoughts haunted me.

We went out on work detachments except for two chaps who volunteered to stay behind to cook and clean. They did that all the time I was there. They had to look after the kitchen and the supplies, which usually came from the village and improvise if there were shortages. Their job included bringing lunch, usually soup, out to us, carrying it in a milk churn on a cart if we weren't working too far away. They had to have supper ready for us when we got back. What we ate depended on what was available.

Monday might be split pea, Tuesday, barley, Wednesday, potato and so on until you came back to the beginning again. Our daily routine was simple. We got up at 6am, had a mug of ersatz coffee (you got used the awful bitter taste of roasted barley) and wash, if it wasn't winter and the tap was frozen. We went out to the farm yard where we assembled in front of the officer who counted us and then divided us up into five teams.

Work schedules were given out – so and so to go there and so and so there, and we walked with our guards out to our various jobs on the farm. Some work lasted weeks, some just days, depending on the season and what was needed. We came back at 6 or 7 in the evening, washed, ate supper, which might be soup or bread and butter and perhaps some sausage and then went to bed. That was the routine pretty much from then onwards.

I was lucky working with the same fellows most of the time. That's when I got to know my four new pals. I think we must have made a good team not to be split up. Sometimes when you first meet somebody, you feel at ease with them and there is an instant bond. It was like that for me and my pals. We shared the same room and our bunks were close together and then we found ourselves out working together. We talked about the usual things men talk about – home, families and jobs. Even though we had different backgrounds and personalities, it didn't matter when we had so much in common: being far from home and loved ones and hating the Germans.

Laurie, Laurence Neville, who came from Presteigne in Radnorshire, was in the Royal Artillery and had been taken prisoner somewhere near Saint-Valery-en-Caux. He was a butcher and his knowledge of animals and ways of killing them was to come in handy. We got on well and liked to share a joke or two. Heb or Hebby, Albert Hebner, who came from Perth, had his head screwed on tight and was always willing to help you out if you were in a bit of bother. There was Sid, Sidney Bentham, who came from St Albans. I wasn't as close to him as the others.

He seemed a bit different, a bit aloof. I think he was from a better class family, possibly even been to public school but we got on all right and he stuck by us.

Then there was Jimmy, James Sellar, who really was the Boss. We none of us could have done without him. He was a great chap. Great, not just because he was tall and well-built, a real asset when you are doing hard physical work together, but his strength of character, common sense and kindness helped see us through the war. He really watched out for us; I'm sure we wouldn't have survived without him.

He was in the Queen's Own Cameron Highlanders and, like Laurie, had been captured at Saint-Valery-en-Caux. When the weather improved he would put on his tartan trousers and black Glengarry cap with red check band. I can picture him now on The Long March, two black ribbons swinging from his cap, as he marched proudly along. He was a gamekeeper on a large estate near Dalwhinnie in the Scottish Highlands and a natural man of action. Which was just as well, because I could hardly understand a word he said in his thick Scottish accent. His resourcefulness and skills proved invaluable throughout our stay and during our long journey to our final liberation.

When people talk about prisoner of war camps now, they have a picture in their mind of Colditz and The Great Escape but I was never an inmate in a place like that, locked up with thousands of other men behind electrified fences, with tall watch towers and patrolling guards. We had no concert parties or officers planning escape routes and digging tunnels. We were an *Arbeitskommando* – a labour battalion, mostly prisoners of war from the lower ranks. It was one of the independent work forces under the command of the main Stalag.

We lived and worked in the local community providing labour for farms, factories, quarries and mines. We were in the middle of nowhere, far from towns or cities, thousands of miles from home, locked in at night, starved of food, worn out by work. We were better off, however, than many of the thousands left behind elsewhere. We were free in our own way in The Great Outdoors. We didn't always have guards breathing down our necks.

Work toughened us up. How do you think I survived those terrible winter months of starvation and marching over 1600km?

People ask me whether I tried to escape. You didn't think of escaping, even if your guard had gone off somewhere to have a smoke and left you standing in the middle of a frozen field with just a spade. Where would you go? You had no money, didn't speak the language, locals weren't particularly friendly, or didn't dare to be, more like. They feared the German officers and guards as much as we did. If you managed to escape and you were caught what would happen to you? I didn't want to think about that as it frightened me more than staying put. Keep your head down, get on with the work, and make the best of it.

Farm work kept us busy. The main crops were wheat, potatoes, cabbages, sugar beet and mangel-wurzels. There was always plenty to do: digging, ploughing, sowing, planting, harvesting; clearing up, cleaning out, cutting down, carrying away. We sifted, sorted, picked and packed. Whatever we were told to do, seven days a week during the summer and six days a week in winter.

Funny how things turn out, finding myself forced to work on a German farm, spending my days handling vegetables, when I'd spent the last ten years lugging them about at market and selling them in the family shop. I didn't like eating my greens back then, but here the only greens I got were stringy bits of cabbage or beet tops in my soup. We were always hungry and on the lookout for something else to eat. What with the hard physical labour we did twelve hours a day, and the poor diet, we were never full and never satisfied.

We didn't start getting Red Cross parcels for quite a while so we kept our eyes skinned for ways of supplementing our diet. Anything. You wouldn't have thought mangel-wurzels which were grown as cattle fodder would be something we craved. But we did.

Mangel-wurzels. Huge, ugly blighters. They didn't taste very nice but they were food and if we were out working and digging them up, we would pocket a few as we went along. We sneaked them into the front of our tunic tops but we couldn't carry many as they bulged and that gave the game away. We took them back, sliced them up, put them on a stick and toasted them in the fire of the wood stove. That is if we were able to get the wretched thing going.

Once the load of logs had gone, which the local farmer supplied to our cooks, we had to do without unless we got some wood ourselves. Hell of a job keeping a fire going if the bits of the twigs and branches we brought back were not dry. The guards weren't bothered what we did; they expected us to find our own fuel if we could. Always on the lookout, not just for food but for anything which might be useful to us. Later on the five of us were on a two months' work detachment in a local forest. Plenty of wood there.

Of course, potatoes were always a favourite. We couldn't get away from them anyway as they were a staple crop. Planting, growing, digging them up and storing them took up a lot of our time. And if we sneaked some back, so much the better although a handful each wasn't much, particularly if you were going to share it with others. So going out on night-time raids for potatoes and other food was another way to supplement our diet. I suppose it was also a bit of an adventure and one-up on our German guards if we were successful.

We found a way of getting out of the camp at night. It all had to be planned carefully. The beauty of it was that we knew if there was anybody about because we could hear the guards' big boots outside or making the floor boards creak if they were nosing around inside. They rarely were; they preferred staying snug inside their quarters. We waited until midnight or one o'clock in the morning when it was all quiet. We were always locked in at night which is why the guards thought we were all safely tucked up in bed. Our house had a set of double doors and the front ones had bolts, which weren't always put across. The inner ones were just locked with a key. If we were lucky we only had one door to deal with and somebody would pick the lock and let out whoever was going out that night.

We decided that it was best if we went out in pairs for safety reasons although, come to think of it now, Jimmy did go off on his own midnight raids. So we sneaked out round the back of our building and through part of the wire fencing we had cut, enough for a man to get through. We folded it back, squeezed through and then folded it back again so nobody could see where the hole was. Favourite places we went to were the storage clamps to get potatoes, which were easy to find because we had built them.

There were four or five clamps in different parts of a field not too far away. What we did to build them was to dig down about 6″ and clear an area about 8″ x 12″ then spread a layer of straw down followed by a layer of potatoes, then more straw and so on. We kept building it up into a big mound and then finally covered it all with earth. The potatoes could be stored for a long time like that. When they were ready to move we dismantled the clamp, digging out the potatoes with special forks with wide prongs, so we didn't spike any and spoil them. We put the potatoes in large baskets which we had brought with us from the farm, carried them to the edge of the field and tipped them into the farm carts. Next day a crowd of us would be sent down to Freystadt railway station where we shovelled them into railway trucks. They then went to factories to make *Kartoffelsalat* – potato salad or *Kartoffelmehl* – potato flour for making dumplings.

We always made the clamps right again so you couldn't see that they had been disturbed. One night Sid and I decided to go out. I remembered this because I was the one who got caught. I had just gone through the hole in the wire and Sid was passing me one of the baskets when we heard the sound of the officer's door opening. Sid grabbed back the basket and together with the other one already in his hand made a run for it back to the house. Unfortunately it was a moonlit night so the guard who had gone outside found me standing a few feet from the fence. He was this little fellow who always carried a revolver and we used to joke that it was bigger than he was. He was obviously proud to be boss tonight. I had a bit of German so I could understand what he said.

'*Was macsht du hier?*' – what are you doing here?

I replied '*Spazierengehen*,' – walking.

He shook his head and said, '*Verboten*' – forbidden. '*Nachts nicht*' – not at night. He paused and thought for a bit. '*Kein Fußball*' – no football. '*Für zwei Wochen*' – two weeks.

That was a pity. What happened was that some of the guards turned a blind eye to us playing a bit of football in the yard, usually in exchange for a packet of twenty Players from our Red Cross parcels when they eventually arrived. It was good to let off steam like this and also good for morale. So we had to do without football for a while and decided to give the midnight excursions a miss for a bit.

I think it was Jimmy found them and told us about some more potatoes. He came across a huge iron drum in a field where local farm workers had been baking potatoes. When he looked inside among the ashes at the bottom he found some left, charred skins, dirt and all. What were they doing there? Some German and Polish farmers used to give the horses some of the waste potatoes if they were short of normal feed. Times were hard for everybody. I hadn't heard of that in this country and I handled horses at home. When we got the chance, and there were no guards checking up, some of us would sneak out with a bucket or bowl, (we could use our caps and pockets too) and fill them up and bring them back. We didn't mind a bit of dirt on our baked potatoes.

None of us liked working for the Germans and helping them in their war effort. Instead of growing crops for the enemy we should have been fighting them and trying to defend our country. Your duty as a prisoner of war is to stop the enemy from getting on with their work as much as you can. So we tried to keep up a spirit of resistance by continuing with small acts of sabotage. While we were picking potatoes for example, and the guard wasn't watching, for every one we picked we trod one into the ground. Seems silly and insignificant now but it meant something to us at the time. Less a victim, more in control.

Another opportunity arose to disrupt our work that seemed safe from repercussions but might be effective; this one was to do with cabbages. Germans were very fond of their sauerkraut and it was an important part of their diet, so keeping a continuous supply of the white cabbages they needed was important to them. We used to work for hours on end in these enormous fields, row upon row of the beastly things. It was back-breaking and exhausting work. We were bending down pulling cabbages out of the hard ground with one hand and with the other, slicing off the bottom with a curved knife. The outer leaves would just fall off the bottom of the cabbage, leaving us with the white centre. These were thrown into nearby baskets and when they were filled, we carried them to the side of the fields and emptied them into the waiting carts. The farm workers or some of our men drove them off to the railway station.

Later on that day or the next, we would march down to the railway sidings just outside Freystadt where wagons were waiting for the cabbages to be loaded so that they could go off to the processing factories like the potatoes. We unloaded them by hand into the covered wagons. When they were full, railway officials would come along and lock them up. The wagons sometimes stayed there overnight before leaving on their long journeys to their destinations all over the country. We hung around knowing this, and when there was nobody about, some of us would sneak onto the tracks again and walk along the wagons looking for holes and gaps in the wooden sides. When we found one, we undid our flies and aiming very carefully, peed through it onto the cabbages inside. With any luck you could get one big jet in which would spray everything inside.

I like to think about the damage we did; that we must have spoilt loads of cabbages which travelled on their long hot journeys to the storage depots and then on to factories for processing. Let them rot. There was a simple satisfaction in sabotaging the sauerkraut. That sort of act of defiance felt good at the time but sadly it was short-lived.

Feelings of helplessness were never far away. We felt this most at times when we witnessed things completely beyond our understanding and our control. You never felt sorry for yourself after the terrible things you saw.

It was probably a few years later in the war that this happened, when we started to hear more about what was happening to the Jews, the political prisoners and minority groups persecuted by the Germans. We knew there was a concentration camp not far away at Stutthof. I saw something terrible happen and I want you to know about it.

I was in a party of about twenty men and we had been sent again to load cabbages at the railway station. As we were working, another train pulling a load of cattle trucks, like the ones we had travelled in, drew up on the opposite line. A large number of German guards appeared and started unbolting and sliding back the doors. I remembered what it felt like inside, hearing that sound, not knowing what was going on and what you would find when you finally got out.

The trucks were packed with people: men, women and children. They were being pulled out by guards and pushed along the tracks. One guard got impatient and grabbed hold of one woman and started yanking her out. She had a little baby in her arms and he snatched it from her. The baby started crying and he threw it onto the ground and started kicking it like a football along the track. The woman screamed and got down and rushed towards her baby bending down to pick it up. The guard shot her in the back of her head. Just one bullet did it. And that tiny baby was just lying there, no longer crying.

Imagine how that made me feel. What could I do? Absolutely nothing. I could only stand and watch. It was frightening. The violence. There was no reason for it. They were wicked. And I felt such anger and hatred. Hatred towards every German in the land.

* * *

There was no time that we prisoners didn't think or talk about food. I used to say, 'When I was in civvy street I couldn't stand mutton stew or tapioca but God give me a bucket of it now.' Were we able to complain about it to anybody? What do you think?

Every once in a while German officers visited from headquarters. They must have been quite high-ranking from the look of them, in their long black leather coats, with a cane in their hand which they kept click clacking on their coats as if to say, 'We're in charge. Watch your step. We've got you here.' They would come and see us working on the farm or visit our billet to check the building and have a look round. I expect they reported back how efficiently run everything was and how well looked after the inmates were. They spoke reasonable English and were able to talk to us or rather address us.

'Is there anything you men want?' they asked.

'Yes, we want more food,' we said.

'Grass is good enough for you people,' they replied.

One of our chaps called Bill (I remember his name because I found out that he lived across the park from me in Barking) had been collecting fleas in a matchbox. Funny what some men do to amuse themselves when they haven't got much entertainment. I suppose he didn't want to waste them once he'd spent all that time picking them off himself. Thought they might come in handy or maybe he was keeping them as pets for a bit of company. I know how important that little mouse was to me when he visited me in my prison cell during my spell in solitary confinement.

As the officers were leaving, Bill somehow managed to sneak up behind them and empty the contents of the matchbox onto the collar and back of their coats. We had a laugh later on, thinking about those officers sitting in their fancy car scratching themselves all the way back to their HQ. And then possibly spreading them to the other officers and then so on through the ranks and right across the whole German Army.

You got used to them. Fleas that is, not the Germans. Never got used to the Germans and what they were capable of doing. But fleas on your body and in your clothes, you had to accept them. Even if you managed get rid of them you would catch more from somebody else soon enough. So you were always scratching and searching your clothes for them. A lot of the time you weren't even aware you were doing it. You would be playing cards or reading a letter from home, pausing to have a good scratch. Sometimes you would pick them off your clothes between your finger nails, squeezing them dead. If it was your turn to have a bath that week you hoped you might drown a load in the water.

There were forty-five of us fighting over one little tin bath – or bowl should I say. We could just about sit in it with our legs dangling over the end. We probably had a bath once a fortnight as it took most of Sunday to get enough hot water from the copper which was always on the go – if we had enough wood for the fire. It was a real palaver when it was Jimmy's turn as he was tall and had to do a sort of Houdini contortionist's act to get himself clean. Two of us usually shared the same water, which soon turned grey with our accumulated dirt. Unless you could be bothered to skim off the black specks of drowned fleas before your turn in the water, you shared those too. We all longed to have a proper shower and dreamed about the time we would.

But I always thought about those poor Jews we had seen and wondered what conditions were like for them in the camps they were being transported to. Of course, after the war I heard the full story about the concentration camps and that 'taking a shower' had another meaning altogether.

7

Bullseye

I always say that it was the International Red Cross who brought us home. Without the British and Canadian food parcels we received, a lot more people would have died. How would we have survived all those years without those extra rations? We thought of them as luxuries but really they were no more than what any ordinary man should have been getting every day. When those shoe boxes started arriving wrapped in brown paper tied with string it was like Christmas. We already had the snow so we were excited like little kids.

We were unlucky where we were, stuck out in the middle of nowhere, as all the consignments of Red Cross parcels were delivered to Stalag 20B. After sorting, our allocation was meant to be sent out to us but, of course, most did not get sent on to us. We never got our fair share. I suppose you can't blame the chaps there for taking some of ours for themselves. Most men in the main camp got theirs once a week or fortnightly while we had to wait as long as seven weeks between deliveries. A basic parcel looked like it had everything a man could want although it was never enough and we often had to share a parcel with somebody else. We usually distributed what we had within our own particular group of friends; we five looked after ourselves.

As a rule we got a packet of tea, sugar and milk, either dried or condensed, and butter. There was some kind of meat like corned beef or streaky bacon, which came out of the tin coiled up in a long strip. There were sardines or pilchards and jam and cheese. There were biscuits, known as pilot biscuits, which were hard and didn't get broken in transit. We had prunes or other dried fruit and always a bar of chocolate, usually Cadbury's fruit and nut. We got extras like mints and jelly, soap and toothpaste and a sewing kit. And plenty of cigarettes, fifty Player's in a round tin.

We all smoked, of course. What else was there to do to relax after a long day out working? But cigarettes were also useful for bartering with the guards for extra food, and occasionally with villagers. It had to be somebody you could trust and you were always careful not to let anybody see you do it. You would give the person twenty ciggies and he would see you got an extra loaf from the village. As they took the cigarettes first, you had to trust that they would come up with the goods. Of course, they could get into serious trouble if the authorities found them fraternising with prisoners so they kept their side of the deal.

When the food was gone, we kept the packaging to use again. We were all good at saving odds and ends for a rainy day. Cardboard boxes were good for storage or could be cut up and used for insulating your clothes and boots. String was useful for hanging up clothes to dry or came in handy at harvest time to tie round your trouser bottoms to keep mice from running up your legs in the hay barn. Empty tins and lids could be bashed out to make tools and containers. A tin of KLIM, the Canadian dried milk (the word Milk spelt backwards) made a good jug, thanks to Heb who got himself a job at the local smithy.

That came about one morning when the *Unteroffizier* asked us at roll call if anybody had worked in a blacksmith's. Heb put his hand up straightaway and said, '*Ja*.' Of course, he'd never been near a smithy in his life but they weren't to know that. You had to use your wits in this place and look for any opportunity that could be turned to your advantage. The local blacksmith needed help because his son had been called up so Heb was taken down there and shown what to do. He was a quick learner and must have been quite good at it because he continued to work there on and off for quite a long time.

At lunchtime the blacksmith went back home for his meal, leaving Heb on his own in the workshop to have the bread and soup which was brought out from the house. He used the time to make things like nails, hooks and kitchen utensils for us depending on what scraps of metal were available. He was treated well there and was always busy with one job or the other for the locals as well as helping us back at camp.

One of our favourite treats from the Red Cross parcels was Rowntree's jelly, which came in cubes. If we got enough packets to make it worthwhile heating up some water and using our precious wood, we made one big one. When we opened our parcels and looked through the contents the shout, 'Jelly!' went up. Once we had three packets, two orange and a lemon, and for some reason my pals gave me the job of making it. It took ages for the water to boil on the wood burning stove as we kept feeding bits of twigs in to keep the fire going. I managed to get enough hot water to melt the jelly. It was winter and the snow was about 18" deep so I thought that it would set nicely outside in my tin bowl.

All the cubes melted and a lovely fruity aroma arose from the bowl as I kept stirring. I carried the hot liquid outside, walking carefully so as not to spill any on the way. I balanced it on a pile of snow outside and then went back in to get warm again. We all forgot about it until Laurie said, 'Chas, when did you last check the jelly?' So off I went back outside only to find that the bowl had turned upside down and there was nothing there. The snow had melted and the bowl had tipped over and all our lovely liquid jelly had disappeared into the ground. Pity I didn't do any science at school or I might have thought of placing the bowl on a piece of wood, even a stone or brick, a surface which didn't conduct heat. Terrible waste of jelly, hot water and fuel! It was a long while before we got any packets of jelly again in our parcels. And when we eventually did it wasn't me asked to make it.

Gradually over time, we received more parcels and some of these came through from home. I wrote to my mother asking for new socks and underwear and a few months later they were delivered. Lily sent me a knitted scarf for my birthday once. It was amazing to think that items like these, requested by thousands of men like me, were able to get across war-torn Europe to us. Fantastic!

My brother-in-law, who was a fireman, sent me one of his jumpers. It was dark blue, in a sort of shiny material which was very warm. Unfortunately, it had a ribbed neck and bottom seam which caused a lot of discomfort to me, not just in the camp but especially on the Long March. Lice like nothing better than a warm, cosy place to settle down and start a family, and seams in clothes are ideal for that. It is, however, almost impossible to find and remove eggs from there. Some people used a lighted match and ran it along a seam to burn them off but it wasn't always successful. Better to be warm and lousy, I believe, than die of cold.

Like all the other men, in all the POW camps everywhere, I treasured every single present I received. I didn't like asking for things from my family. Even though they weren't luxuries or treats but essentials, I always felt bad about my mother having to send stuff out to me. I was worried all the time. I didn't know what she and other members of the family were really going through. Letters were always cheerful and didn't tell me what was really happening at home. Was the family safe? Was the shop doing OK? How were they managing for money? I felt useless. Lily had a career of her own now because she knew that I might not come back. Not that she said that exactly in her letters but joining the ATS got her away from her family and helped her become financially independent. If only I had some proper money I could send home.

Who needs money when you're stuck in the back of beyond with nothing to spend it on? What would be the point of paying wages for the work we did? So why would they give us this paper money which could only used in a POW camp? It might be OK for fellows in the big camps who could buy razor blades and soap but there was nothing here. You could gamble with it, use it to roll your own cigarettes or it might come in handy to wipe your bottom if you were caught short somewhere. Cigarettes were our main currency.

The German government introduced a system of payment to prisoners of war for the work they did in the labour camps. It was called *Kriegsgefangenen Lagergeld* – prisoner of war camp money, and they paid 'wages' with these little tiny notes like doll's house money – about the size of a cigarette card. This currency was only valid within a POW camp so it was pretty useless. What's the point of winning a game of Rummy or Sevens and having a handful of these *Reichspfennigs* at the end of a game?

One day some of us were playing cards and Heb was doing well, collecting notes from us each time he won a hand. A guard came into the room to see what we were doing as he heard all this cheering (and booing) after another of his wins. This particular guard was a decent sort of chap, one of those you could talk to: us with our pidgin German and him with his hand signals. He watched us playing for a moment before coming over. I think he had his eye on Hebby's winnings on the table and asked us what we were going to do with the money.

'Nichts,' – nothing, we said, '*Nichts zu kaufen,'* – nothing to buy.

'*Magst du Musik?'* – do you like music? The guard started to mime playing the piano.

'*Ja, ja,*' we said, wondering why he'd asked. And Jack, who was very musical and could play the piano, came forward and repeated, '*Ja. Ja. Musik,*' running his fingers up and down an imaginary keyboard. '*Ich liebe Musik,*' – I love music. 'The piano. *Das piano?*'

'*Ach ja. Das Klavier,*' – oh yes, the piano, the guard corrected. '*Schön,*' – lovely, he said.

Jack nodded. '*Ja, das Klavier. Schön,*' and looked at us all. We nodded in agreement, not sure where all this was leading. '*Musik. Ich liebe,*' we chorused.

The guard smiled and started miming playing a piano accordion, moving his arms about as though pushing bellows in and out. '*Sie möchte,*' – you would like, pointing at Jack, '*ein Akkordeon?*'

Everybody said '*Ja, ja,*' looking at each other, '*Ein Akkordeon. Ja,* ' wondering if the guard had gone mad. I couldn't believe it; he was asking us if we would like an accordion. How on earth could he get us an instrument or anything like that? Perhaps he had one at home he wanted to get rid of and saw an opportunity or he had a friend who could get one.

But I couldn't see what he or any shopkeeper would do with our camp money, which was worthless.

A few days later the guard came back. He said he had been to a shop in the town to find out how much they wanted for the instrument and he named an amount. Let's say it was 1000 *Reichsmark* and we said '*Ja, ja,*' again, and collected up all the money we could find and handed it over. He came back the next day carrying an enormous parcel, properly wrapped up in paper with string round it. He hadn't tried to hide it and nobody had stopped him on the way into the camp. We pushed Jack forward to receive it. 'Go on, it's for you,' and 'you can play.'

When he opened the parcel and saw the lovely accordion his face lit up. It must be terrible for somebody with a special talent or skill to be stuck in a place like that with no way of practising it. He immediately started opening and closing the accordion, breathing some life into it. He managed to play a few scales and we all clapped. It was wonderful to hear a sound like that after being starved of music for so long. From then on Jack practised regularly and we enjoyed listening to him.

As he got better, he played all sorts of music to cheer us all up. We were thrilled that nobody stopped him. Perhaps the guards got some pleasure from hearing the sound of the accordion wafting over to their quarters or they just thought if we were listening to it in our spare time then we couldn't be getting up to any mischief. We had singsongs together in the evening and sometimes some of the fellows danced around together, no doubt imagining they were holding the sweetheart they had left behind. It almost made me want to dance. But I didn't.

The question of proper wages arose again later when a fellow joined our camp in exchange for one of our men who had gone off sick. We were sitting round talking about money one evening, saying how worried we were about our families. There were a few married men with children among us, so obviously the main bread winner of their family was absent from home. This fellow told us that we could send money home to our families.

'But we haven't got any money,' somebody said.

'Of course you have. Your army pay is still being paid into your bank at home.'

We hadn't thought of that. 'That's no good with us stuck here,' said another.

'Now I've done this myself,' he said. 'You can write from here to your paymaster and send it with your normal camp mail. You ask them for such and such an amount to be sent to whoever you want to. And Bob's your uncle.'

I couldn't believe it but then decided that there was nothing to lose so I might as well have a go. When we were given our next supply of camp writing paper, I did exactly that. I didn't know the address but marked it to The Paymaster, c/o The War Office, London, England. I had no idea how much I had in the account but I asked for £100 to be forwarded to my parents. Two or three months later, I had a letter from my mother thanking me for the money. I was amazed that it had worked and tried it again, sending them another £100. My only thought was that they could be in trouble and I wanted to help. Money was no use to me in there and I never thought about needing it when I got home. I didn't plan for the future; I just lived from day to day.

When I finally got home after the war, my parents had kept the money for me and paid it all back. That was why I could afford to buy Lily an enormous 18 carat gold diamond engagement ring on my return.

* * *

As the months slipped by and then the years, we settled into our life in the camp. We had our work and we had our leisure time – evenings and Sundays. Much of that was taken up with our own little jobs such as washing and mending clothes, darning socks and pants and writing letters. We also socialised, playing football and cards and listening to Jack play. But even this got monotonous. I know some camps received books and board games, they even had records and gramophones but not where I was. We had to make our own entertainment, which wasn't easy. It was important to have an outlet for our anger and frustrations and also good to have a laugh and a bit of fun.

Many of the other prisoners were good with their hands and had a wealth of experience from civilian life. We had a tailor, a chap who lived not far from me in Barking, who was able to make things like hats and mittens out of bits of old uniform. He made me a smart new cap which I liked to wear as it wasn't army regulation. We had a cobbler who helped us mend our boots with leather patches which came in some of the Red Cross parcels. He made me a belt out of the tops of old army boots. Laurie, the butcher, knew about animals, looking after and killing them; Jimmy, the gamekeeper, loved the outdoor life and was knowledgeable about birds and plants. There was Heb, on his way to becoming a proper blacksmith. My ability to contribute was limited as I didn't have any special skills and had never been apprenticed to a trade or profession. Being able to add up the price of a pound of potatoes and half a pound of carrots wasn't much use here. So I hoped the opportunity would arise for me to help out in some way.

At roll call one morning, the *Unteroffizier* read out the work schedule. He needed a group of men for forestry work. Eight of us, including me and three of my pals, were allocated a two months' work detachment in the Rosenberg Forest region, working under the jurisdiction of a local forest ranger. Although it wasn't too far away from the camp, we were working in a large area of forest and could cover a lot of ground during the day. So we had to take our own food with us for the day. The soup cart wouldn't be able to come out to us. It was a welcome break from the farm and the change of scene and different type of work gave us greater freedom. Another lucky break for me.

We had to walk about 5km to the working site and one of guards escorted us as far as a clearing, bang in the middle of this vast conifer forest. We knew then that we had come to somewhere special. It was beautiful and so quiet, just bird song and wind rustling the tops of the pine trees. The guard left us when the forest ranger appeared, a chap dressed all in green with a sort of Tyrolean hat and feather sticking out.

Private Charles Waite, Queen's Royal Regiment, October 1939.

Winnie in the family shop *c.*1930.

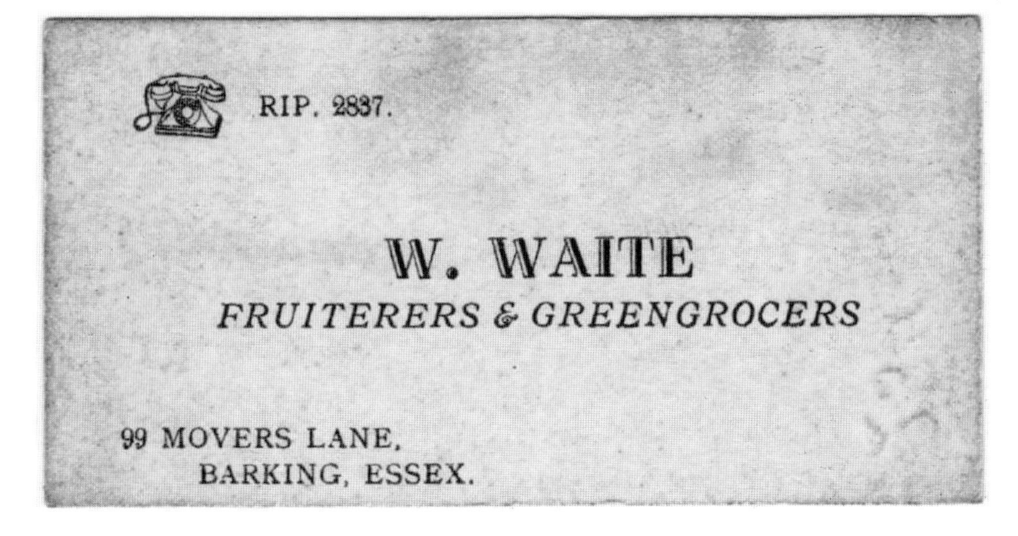

Family business card.

Charles, aged nine, on the delivery vehicle with his brothers Reginald and Alfred.

Charles aged twelve with Peter the dog.

Waite family at Reg's wedding, 1933. Charles carried this photograph throughout the war.

Back row: Leonard (20), Doris (22), Muriel (16), Alf (28), Winnie (18), Marjorie (26), Reg (24).

Front row: Elsie (11), William and Alice (parents), Charles (14).

Lily's parents, Alf and Ada Mathers.

Lily Mathers, 1938. Charles carried this photograph throughout the war.

The BEF lands in France. How many of these men would make it out of Dunkirk?

Up to their necks in it. A human chain from shore to ship at Dunkirk.

Stalag XX (20)B stamp on the reverse of the photograph of Lily.

Kriegsgefangenenlager STALAG XXA (3A) Datum 26.6.40
Prisoner of War Camp 8560 Date
Name Waite Vorname Charles H
Surname Christian Name
Dienstgrad u. Truppenteil (Private) Queens Royal Regiment
Rank and Unit
Geburtsdatum May 8th 1919 Geburtsort England
Date of birth Native place
Letzter Wohnort 99 Movers Lane London.
Last dwelling
Adresse meiner Angehörigen 99 Movers Lane
Home Address Barking, Essex, England.
Unverwundet – leicht verwundet – in deutsche Kriegsgefangenschaft geraten –
Unwounded – slightly wounded – prisoner of war in Germany –
... mich wohl.
... am well.
Nichtzutreffendes ist zu streichen
(Passages not appropriate to the point to be cancelled)
Charles Waite
Signature

Copy of Charles's signed admission card to Stalag XX(20)A dated 26 June 1940 (International Red Cross).

Red Cross advertisement. A Surrey vicar 'adopted' Charles as his own POW and sent cigarettes in bulk, useful to barter with for food.

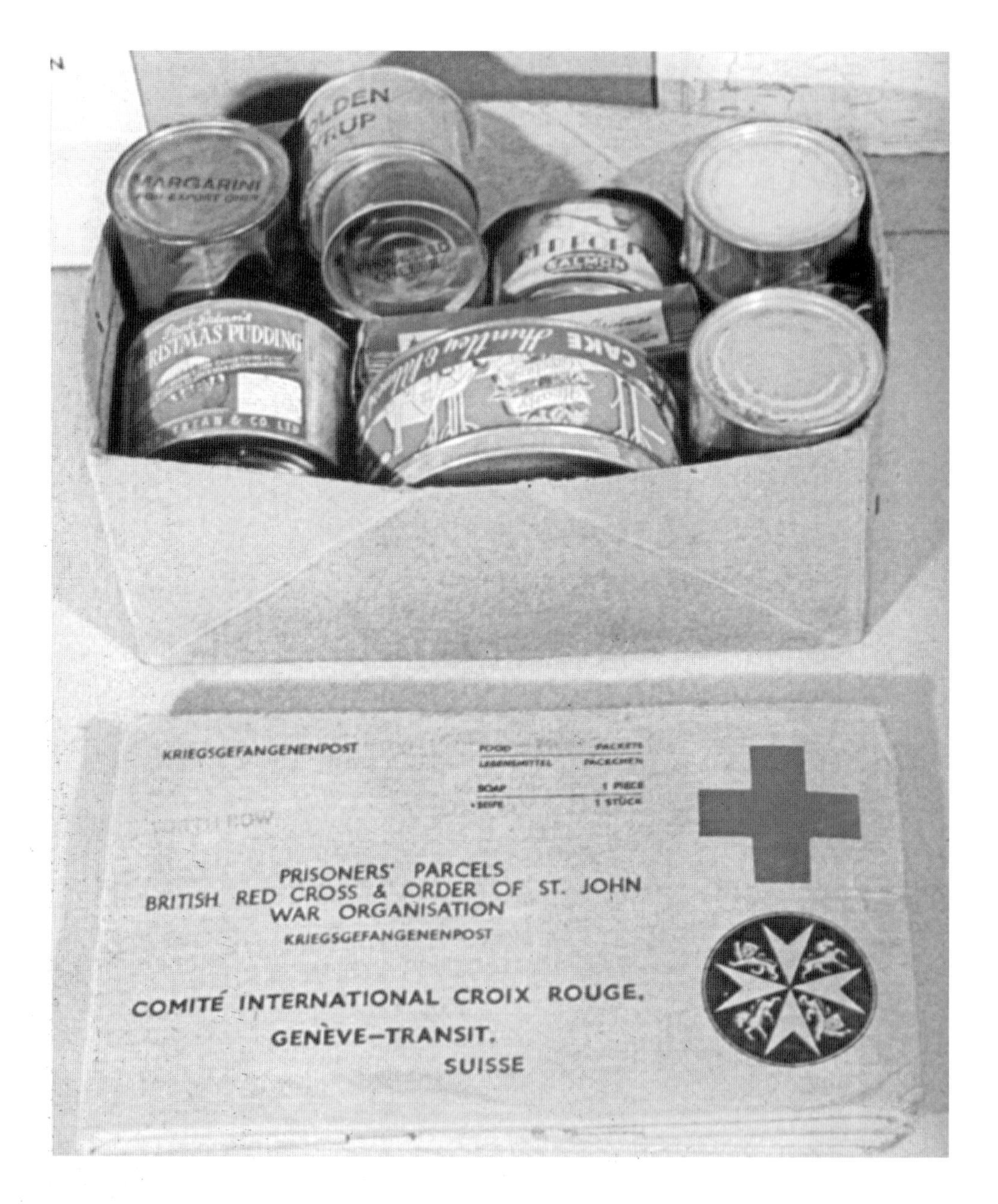

A Red Cross parcel issued to prisoners of war.

Piles of food packages at the International Red Cross warehouse in Geneva, in a photograph probably taken late in the war. (Library of Congress)

A *Hilfswillige* (volunteer helper) armband printed with the words: 'In Service of the German armed forces'. These were worn by Russian prisoners of war, used by the German Army for slave labour.

Charles's PoW camp dog tag No: 10511 issued at Stalag 20A Thorn.

Private Charles Waite on the Stalag 20B farm, 1941.

Kriegsgefangenenlager Datum 5TH April. 1942.

Dear Winnie & Bert, Pleased to be receiving your letters. I am afraid we have no concerts as there are just seven of us but we get along very well. It is nice to know you all go to dances and I wish I were able to. (But I cannot dance). Cheerio for now. Your Loving Brother Charlie xxx

'I cannot dance' camp letter from Charles to Winnie and Bert, 5 April 1942.

Kriegsgefangenenlager Datum: 23rd Jan. 1944

Dear Mrs Goldsmith, Very many thanks for your kindness and a very nice surprise. I received the cigarettes quite safely yesterday. I hope you and all are well. When you write to Charlie, give him my regards and best wishes. I'm sure it can't be far off now; and then I hope to thank you personally. I hope you'll excuse me for not writing often, our writing material is rationed. Best Wishes and Kindest Regards. Tommy H.

Tommy Harrington's letter to Winnie, 22 January 1944.

Kriegsgefangenenlager
Camp des prisonniers

Datum: 18 Nov. 1941.
date

Dear Win & Bert. Hope you are keeping well. Thank Reg for his letter which I received this week and greatly appreciate. Keep smiling and have as good a Christmas as you can under the circumstances. Remember me, & give my love to all. Charlie

Kriegsgefangenenpost
Correspondance des prisonniers de guerre
Postkarte Carte postale

Stalag XX B
Geprüft 13a

Mrs. A. Goldsmith

Gebührenfrei! Franc de port!

Absender:
Expéditeur:
Vor- und Zuname: CHARLES WAITE
Nom et prénom
Gefangenennummer: 10511
No. du prisonnier
Lager-Bezeichnung: Stalag XX B
Nom du camp
Deutschland (Allemagne)

Empfangsort: Ilford (Essex)
Lieu de destination
Straße: 47, Meadway
Rue
Land: England.
Landesteil (Provinz usw.)
Dépt.

Letter and envelope sent from camp, March 1944.

Envelope received from home, April 1944.

Group camp photograph, 1941 (GB 1373). Charles stands third from right in the back row, Jimmy fourth. Heb is first from left in the front row, Laurie third.

Group camp photograph, 1942 (GB 557). Heb stands first from left on the back row, Charles fifth. Laurie is in the middle of the front row.

'The Russians are coming.' It was the successes of the Red Army that created the suffering of The Long March.

Notes written during The Long March on the back of Charles's camp propaganda postcard.

(MARCH. 16.)

NEARLY 8 WEEKS ON THIS NIGHTMARE MARCH.
NOW LYING IN BARNS WAITING TO MOVE AGAIN.
RATIONS VERY BAD. EVERYBODY HUNGRY & WEAK.
OUR PLANES ARE BOMBING EVERY DAY & NIGHT.
TODAYS DINNER (FEW SPUDS IN JACKETS).
BOILED BARLEY & MEAT FOR TEA.
(ABOUT 10 LB BARLEY & 5 LB MEAT) 100 MEN
SID. LAURIE & MYSELF JUST DELOUSED.
THINGS LOOK VERY BAD FOR US.
WE KNOW THERE IS A LOT OF RED X
~~ME~~ LYING SOMEWHERE BUT WE CAN'T
GET IT. JERRY HAS NO TRANSPORT.
WE HOPE SOMETHING WILL SOON TURN UP.
IF NOT. "GOD HELP US"

(MARCH. 30.)

THINGS 100% WORSE.
HAVE ARRIVED AT A PLACE (STENDAL)
LIVING IN HORSE STALLS. (1000 MEN)
WORKING ON BOMBED AREA (STATION)
CLEARING UP. TWO MORE OF OUR
MEN HAVE PASSED AWAY. WE
ARE BADLY IN NEED OF FOOD
A BATH & CLOTHING.
SID COLLAPSED AT WORK AND
ALSO OTHERS. THE GUARDS ARE
INHUMAN. HAVE SEEN QUITE
A NUMBER OF YANKS NOW
AND THEY LOOK PRETTY BAD.
SOME WERE IN ENG., XMAS.

(MARCH 31. YANKS BILLET BOMBED.)

Notes and map written in the New Testament received on the Long March, 28 January 1945.

"THE MARCH" (1945)
RUSSIAN ARMY PUSHES FORWARD AND WE EVACUATE.

39 MEN.
LEFT THE FARM "LANGENAU" (JAN 20) 2 MEN STAY IN HIDING.
EVERYBODY IN GOOD SPIRITS. A FAIR SUPPLY OF RED CROSS AND ONLY
EXPECT FEW DAYS MARCHING. (JAN 21) MARCH 42 KLM. NEARLY ALL
OF US THROW AWAY A LOT OF KIT. MUCH TO HEAVY TO CARRY.
SLEEPING IN BARNS AT NIGHT AND MAKING OUR OWN FIRES
FOR RED CROSS COOKING + TEA. SPEND A NIGHT ON THE
ROAD SIDE. BITTER COLD. MAKE TEA WITH SNOW.
5 OF US MUCKING IN. LAURIE. SID. HEB. JIMMY + MYSELF.
THINGS GETTING VERY BAD. SOAKING WET AT NIGHT
SLEEP IN BARNS. MANY OF THE LADS ILL. GUARDS ARE
GETTING VERY BAD. AS THE DAYS ROLL ON IT GETS
WORSE. EATING RAW TURNIPS. WORSE THAN 1940 MARCH.
HEB DROPS OUT SICK.

(EASTER SUNDAY.)
MUCH WORSE NOW. 3 HAVE DIED.
SID COLLAPSED. TAKEN TO STALAG.
RATIONS VERY POOR. WE ARE WORKING.
VERY, VERY LITTLE CHANCE OF RED CROSS.

'God Help Us' Letter, January–April 1945.

Kriegsgefangenen-Lagergeld 4·3331046
Gutschein über 1 Reichspfennig
Dieser Gutschein gilt nur als Zahlungsmittel für Kriegsgefangene und darf von ihnen nur innerhalb der Kriegsgefangenenlager oder bei Arbeitskommandos in den ausdrücklich hierfür bezeichneten Verkaufsstellen verausgabt und entgegengenommen werden. Der Umtausch dieses Gutscheines in gesetzliche Zahlungsmittel darf nur bei der zuständigen Kasse der Lagerverwaltung erfolgen. Zuwiderhandlungen, Nachahmungen und Fälschungen werden bestraft.
Der Chef des Oberkommandos der Wehrmacht
Im Auftrage:

1 1
DEUTSCHES REICH
WIEN 62
10.XI.44
2b

Example of *lagergeld* – camp money.

2

(I) SOLDIER'S NAME and DESCRIPTION on ATTESTATION.

Army Number 6092950
Surname (in capitals) WALTE
Christian Names (in full) CHARLES HENRY
Date of Birth 8-5-1919
Place of Birth. Parish Barking
In or near the town of London
In the county of
Trade on Enlistment Greengrocer Asst.

Nationality of Father at birth British
Nationality of Mother at birth – –
Religious Denomination C of E
Approved Society NI
Membership No.
Enlisted at Horsham On 18-10-39
For the :—
* Regular Army. * Supplementary Reserve.
* Territorial Army. * Army Reserve Section D.
* Strike out those inapplicable.
Duration
For .... years with the Colours and .... years in the Reserve.

~~Particulars of former service Army No., Corps or Regiment and period.~~

Signature of Soldier C H Waite.
Date 18-10-39

3

DESCRIPTION ON ENLISTMENT.

Height 5 ft. 7 ½ ins. Weight 130 lbs.
Maximum Chest 34 ins. Complexion Fair
Eyes Blue Hair Fair
Distinctive Marks and Minor Defects Nil

CONDITION ON TRANSFER TO RESERVE.

Found fit for
Defects or History of past illness which should be enquired into if called up for Service

Date .... 19 ....
Initials of M.O. i/c ....

A 2

Charles's Army Book 64 – Soldier's Service and Pay Book – which he kept with him throughout the war.

Lily in an ATS group photograph, taken while she was stationed at Slough, 1944. She is in the second row from the front, fourth from left.

Manufacturers of the
[Cel]ebrated "Magno" Watch

Licensed Valuers for
Probate, etc.

[E]STABLISHED AT
[4]76 OXFORD ST., LONDON, W.1
371 STRAND, LONDON, W.C.2
[.]3 TOTTENHAM COURT RD., LONDON, W.1
89 LORD ST., LIVERPOOL, 2
[.]7 PICCADILLY, MANCHESTER, 1
37 MARKET ST., MANCHESTER, 1
25 GALLOWTREE GATE, LEICESTER
37 BROAD ST., READING

Herbert Wolf Ltd

Goldsmiths and Jewellers
476 OXFORD ST., LONDON, W.1 TELE[PHONE / GRAPH] MUSEUM 7266 EXT. 1

M ....

Date 13/6/45 Sold by 90 – 56

Dia Cluster
Ring £38/10/-
(18ct.)

F 12817

REPAIRS A SPECIALITY
ESTIMATES FREE

Receipt for Lily's engagement ring, 13 June 1945.

Charles and Lily on their wedding day, 25 June 1945.

Charles as best man at Laurie Neville and Connie's wedding.

Lily, Charles and Brian, Cliftonville, 1949.

Lily, Charles and Brian, 1950.

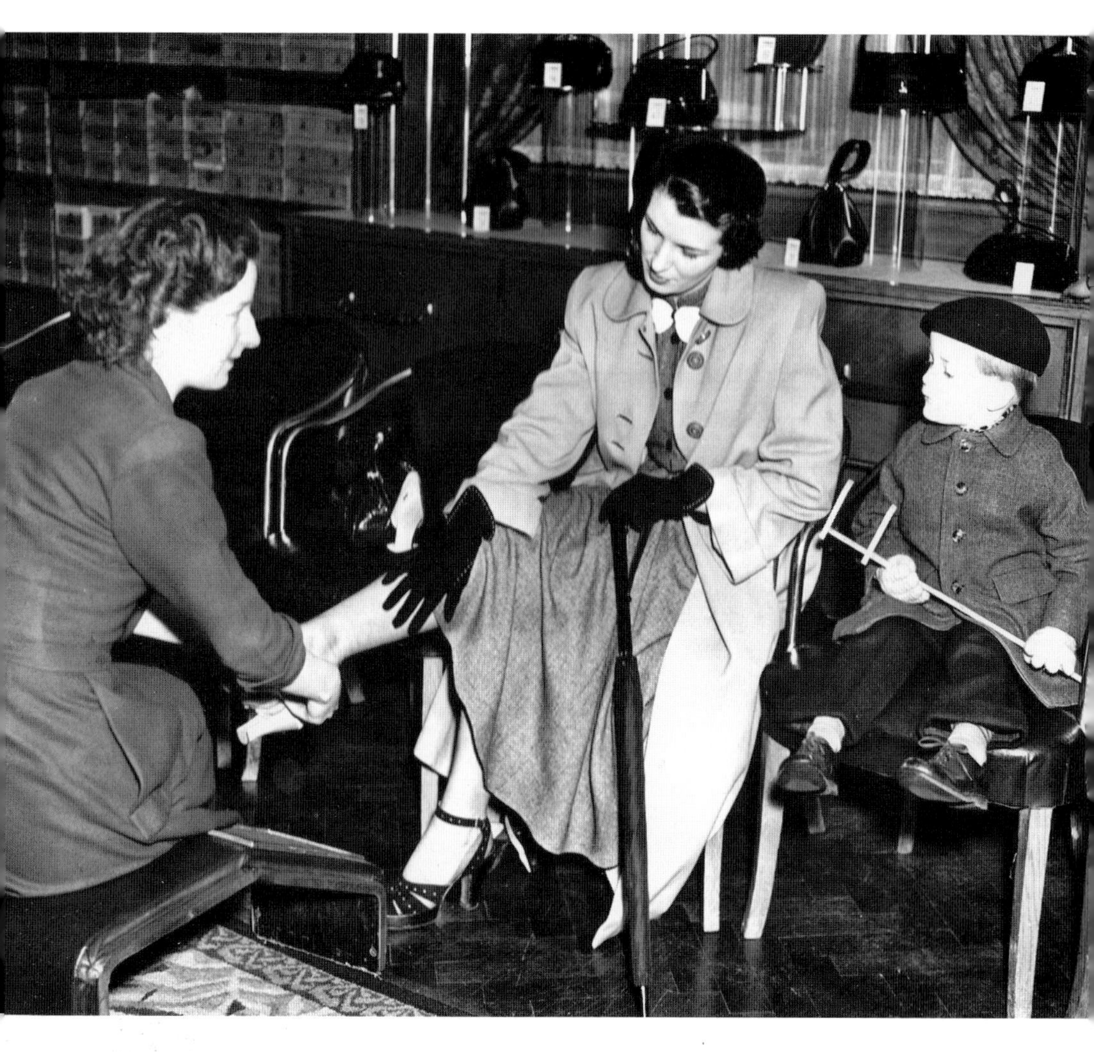

Brian models for Dolcis Shoe Shop advertisement, Romford, February 1951.

Lily sewing, *c*.1980.

Charles on train to York, 1980.

Brian's graduation, Liverpool University, 1968.

Brian with keyboard
*c.*1980.

Charles at 'Captured: The Extraordinary Life of Prisoners of War' exhibition at the Imperial War Museum North, May 2009.

Charles with Terry Waite, CBE at the opening of 'Captured: The Extraordinary Life of Prisoners of War' exhibition at the Imperial War Museum North, May 2009.

On the road to Abbeville. Charles in France with Testimony Films, for the documentary *Dunkirk: the Forgotten Heroes*, Discovery Channel, 2010.

Charles attends a Buckingham Palace Garden Party, July 2010.

Charles with Allan M. Jones at USAF Lakenheath, September 2010.

92nd birthday visit to the National Memorial Arboretum, 8 May 2011.

Charles with niece Valerie Wood, left, and her sons Martin & Christopher at wreath laying at the NEXPOWA Memorial Gates.

Reisenburg, Kreis Rosenberg from Bildarchiv Ostpreussen.de.

Colonel John T. Quintas (left), 48th Fighter Wing commander, with Charles and ex-POW Tony Hawkins after a ceremony honouring prisoners of war and those missing in action, USAF Lakenheath, September 2011. (Courtesy USAF, photo by Airman Cory D. Payne)

'The Last Ordeal' by Doris Allan.

He carried a bayonet, not as a weapon, but to mark the trees for cutting down. He told us a bit about the types of trees in the forest and the work of a forester, in his broken English mixed with a lot of arm waving and hand gestures.

There were mainly pines, firs and spruce and he pointed to some logs piled up ready for collection. '*Holz*,' – wood, he said. We nodded. '*Für Mäntel*', – for coats, he was stroking the front of his jacket. We looked surprised. '*Ja*, for ze clothes.' I couldn't believe it but it was true. He showed us the equipment, a couple of cross-cut saws and some choppers, pretty basic, and demonstrated how to cut and fell a tree, chip off any smaller lower branches and saw the trunks into the required lengths for stacking and then transportation later.

For some reason he chose me to record how much we did each day. He gave me a notebook and pencil to keep a tally of the wood we cut down. We measured areas off in square metres, marking them out with small poles. Four men worked on one area and four on another until we'd done ten metres. But instead of writing ten down, I would write eight which I thought would give us a bit of slack if we had a bad day or needed to take it easy on another. Then we could add those two onto another day to make it up. We had targets to reach and the ranger trusted us to do a good job. He didn't have the time himself to stand around in the cold counting all the timber we had cut and stacked. So we did a good job as we did not want to get into trouble. We liked it out there; we didn't feel as though we were under the thumbs of the German authorities.

The ranger went off and left us to it, returning from time to time to check on our progress. It was hard work but we were our own masters pretty much, enjoying the freedom we had. We could stop and have a break when we liked. We always carried our bowls and spoons and we had brought some food with us, bit of bread and butter saved from the night before, maybe something left from a Red Cross parcel to make a small meal. As we were miles from anywhere, we were able to build a little fire to keep ourselves warm and we melted a bit of snow in a bowl, added a few tea leaves which we had saved in a twist of paper and put in a pocket before leaving the camp. Bob's your uncle – a nice cuppa cha!

Jimmy was in his element. I suppose he imagined he was back on his Drumochter Estate. As game-keeper, he was responsible for the shoot and looked after the birds and organised the beaters. He was a very good shot and told us about taking part in national competitions down at Bisley. It was pity he didn't have a gun there; we could have done with a bird or two for the pot for supper. Instead Jimmy talked about life on the country estate where he worked and the changing seasons and the beauty of a life outdoors. He pointed out trees and plants to us and identified bird calls as we sat in a clearing warming our hands by the fire.

I remember going to see Jimmy in the Highlands of Scotland in 1960, driving with Lily and our son Brian, in our first new car, a Ford Consul, which cost £600. Jimmy wasn't expecting us and I didn't know his address exactly but enquired when we got to a village near where I thought he lived. I asked at the post office if they knew him and sure enough I was directed to his cottage nestling in a hillside. Fortunately his wife, Catherine, was home but Jimmy was working up on the hills. She went outside to the back of the house and gave a loud whistle through two fingers which was some sort of signal. A moment later we heard a whistle answering back from far away and she replied to that with a different whistle. When Jimmy eventually appeared, carrying a dead lamb over his arm, he not only he knew to come home, because he had visitors, but also to bring something to put in the pot for supper.

We quite often glimpsed deer through the trees while we were there but they were shy creatures and we never got really close to any. One day, however, I was sitting quietly on my own on a tree trunk when an adult male deer, a lovely russet colour with dapples of cream on its back, emerged from the trees and stopped at the edge of the road running through the forest. He looked from side to side and when he saw that it was all clear and there was obviously no danger, he stamped his little hooves on the ground to signal to the others that it was safe. A whole herd appeared, mothers and babies and all, and followed him off into the safety of the forest again. Moments of solitude and beauty like this were precious then. They helped restore your spirit and give you the strength to carry on.

Of course, we took advantage of our time in the forest to collect kindling wood and bring back what we could for the stove. But one day, I had another idea. As we were measuring up a trunk for cutting up into the required lengths, I remarked that a piece of that would make a good dartboard. I think it was the rings inside that reminded me of the score board with the bullseye in the middle. The others agreed it was a terrific idea and it would cheer the other chaps up. I thought it would make a change from playing cards or our homemade snakes and ladders. Football was impossible in bad weather so some indoor competition would be good. 'OK, Chas, over to you.'

I was getting quite good at this woodcutting caper so I sawed off a section. Boy, was it heavy! So I took off my overcoat and wrapped the block in it and carried it like that. Our guard who came back to collect us did not say anything when he saw me in just my tunic and trousers. I thought he would think, 'What's he doing without his coat on a cold day like this?' It was freezing cold. But he was only interested in getting us back as fast as he could so he could get back into the warm and enjoy a plate of *Bratwurst* and tot of schnapps. So I carried the block of wood wrapped up in my overcoat all the way back to camp. At last I had something to contribute. When I showed Heb the piece of wood and explained about turning it into a dart board he said he could do that.

The next time he went to the blacksmith's shop to work, Heb saw a man's bicycle leaning up against a wall outside. When nobody was about, he removed some spokes from the wheels. Because they were long he had to fold them in half to get them in his jacket pocket in order to sneak them back. We used the spokes to make the rings and the numbers on the darts board. The chap who was making the darts whittled down bits of wood for the body and cut bits off a spoke to use as the tip. There were plenty of chicken feathers floating around the place so he had no problem making the flights and between us we managed to make a dozen darts. The dart board went down really well with everybody and we even started a league table for different teams in the dormitories.

Unfortunately, during one of the inspections, the officers turned up and found them and confiscated the darts and the board. '*Verboten*,' – forbidden. And holding up a dart as though it was a deadly weapon. '*Nein. Nein. Schlecht*.' – No, no, bad. But a month later we made another board and started playing again. Heb was still working at the blacksmiths shop and he had enough spokes left to make another lot.

It was important to keep up morale with activities like this and also to be able to get one over on the Germans. The feeling of victory, however small, felt good but sadly did not last. You never knew what was round the corner to bring you down with a bump again.

One time we were sent out to help a local farmer with muck spreading. It took a couple of days to cover the acres and acres of land. Farm workers had been collecting manure in their carts for a while from all over the place, stables, cattle sheds and pigsties, I imagine, and transporting it to the fields to deposit in heaps ready for us. We came along in our work parties with our spades and worked slowly spreading the stuff over the ground. We were working in a field near a large farmhouse when we heard the sound of an engine as it came along the road towards us. Anything like that was of interest. It was such an isolated place we wanted to know what was going on. Was it someone coming to check up on us? Then we saw this big, black, shiny official-looking car approaching, which pulled up on the road outside the farmhouse.

Two German officers got out. I'm sure they were SS from how they were dressed in their sharp uniforms, shiny, high boots and the way they carried themselves, stiff backed and marching purposefully. They went towards the house where a Polish couple lived with their son, whom we learned later had already been taken off to a concentration camp. They banged on the door. When it opened they pushed in and we heard a woman scream and a terrific row going on. The officers came out dragging a man down the front steps. He was struggling and shouting, and the more he did, the more tightly the officers either side held him. His wife was screaming and trying to stop the men taking her husband.

The officers had originally intended to take the man away, I believe, but they decided it was not worth all the trouble. One of them let go of him and came across the road and started walking towards us. Oh, God, what's going on? They're coming for us now. I looked down briefly so that I didn't catch the other man's eyes. One of our guards went across to meet the officer to find out what he wanted. They spoke for a moment and then our chap came back towards us and took spades from the two nearest of our fellows. He then joined the officer and walked onto the road and went with him. As the other officer held the man down, they set about beating him again and again about the head until he fell to the ground in a heap. The officers got back in their car and drove off leaving the man dead on the ground. Our guard came back with the spades and we carried on working.

Next morning on our way back to finish our work in the fields, we had to walk past the body, which was still lying on the road side, unrecognisable now as a fellow human being.

8

Postcard Home

Post early for Christmas, that's what they tell you nowadays. It's a pity that my family didn't think of that during the war because I usually got my Christmas cards and letters in February. Of course, my family didn't know what was going on where I was and I didn't tell them.

We only had a fortnightly allowance of four or five sheets of camp writing paper and one card, and with so little space you didn't want to waste your words. All anybody wanted to know was that we were OK and we wanted to know the same about them. So messages both ways were simple and cheerful. You couldn't have said what you really thought anyway.

Letters were censored. We had to be careful what we wrote and anything directly about the war was avoided so we sometimes tried to sneak things in. I wrote to my oldest brother Alfred, about the time of the invasion of Sicily, saying, 'I was pleased to hear about Auntie Cissie,' which was supposed to be my code. When I got home, I remembered to ask Alfred about it and he said that he hadn't received that particular letter. I wasn't surprised.

I had a lot of family to write to and some of them wrote back regularly. I'm sorry to say that my father wasn't one of them. He only wrote twice, possibly three times, in all those five years. In one of his letters he told me that he now owned two cars – an Austin A40 and a Rover, and he promised me one of them when I returned after the war. That was nice, I thought, something to look forward to. I missed driving.

Sad to say, once I was home he never mentioned the car again and I never got one. As I found out, even after all I had been through, nobody in the family was going to give me a helping hand. I missed out on all those years when they were building up the family business, having children and buying their own homes. In the end, I had to make my own way in the world with just Lily by my side.

Lily, mum and my sister Winnie were the main ones who wrote. Winnie kept all my letters to her and Bert, her husband, which was good as I can read them again and think back to what was going on at the time.

6 September 1942

Dear Win & Bert, I have not heard from you for a long time & I wondered if it was because I do not write myself. I am sure you understand that my writing material is rationed and I like Lily & Mum to hear from me as often as possible so I apologise for not writing. Cheerio for now. Love Charlie xxx

9 January 1944

Sorry I cannot write more often but as you know writing material is limited and naturally it is my wish to correspond with Lily and Mum as often as is possible … PS just received your cigs. Your Loving Brother Charlie xxxx

But the truth is that my letters don't tell me much now about what was happening to me and what I really felt. All they show is that I was worried about everybody at home, particularly my mother. I didn't want to upset her after all she had been through. A month or so after I left for France to go to war, she received a letter from The War Office: 'We regret to tell you that your son is missing in France'. My poor mother! It was quite a while before she got another letter telling her that I was alive and safe, and a prisoner of war; that was all it said.

Later on she was given the address to send letters to me but I don't expect she had a clue where or what *M Stammlager XXB (129) Deutschland* was. Mother wrote the most and included messages from other members of the family. She also sent the parcels, mainly of extra items of clothing such as a pair of new boots, socks and that jumper from Bert, my fireman brother-in-law. Letters could take two to three months to get to you and the same for your letters going back to England.

It was fantastic returning to camp at 7 o'clock in the evening or maybe 8 in summer, everybody gradually coming in from their various work detachments, tired, dirty and hungry, to be greeted by the cry, 'Mail up!' We were so excited. It meant so much to us to get post from home and we would rush to collect what there was for us. Letters used to arrive all together so you could have a bunch of half a dozen to put in date order so you could read them in sequence and make sense of the news. You didn't want to read about of the arrival of a new nephew before you had even heard that your sister was expecting. And you read them over and over again and looked after them, folding them carefully each time and putting them back in your shoebox. Each one was a life saver.

I was very upset when I threw all my letters away soon after setting out on The March in January 1945. I kept two envelopes, one from my mother and one from Lily, that was all. We could only carry essentials such as food and clothing. Lily's letters were special to me and I wish I still had them now she's no longer with me.

I always felt sorry for the lads who didn't have anybody to write to when I collected my bundle and took it back to my room to read in a quiet corner. It was a comfort to see familiar handwriting and to read family news, how everybody was and what new additions there were to the family:

18 July 1943

Dear Winnie and Bert, Pleased to hear the good news and I hope you are both satisfied. (I would be) I expect to hear from you soon. You said you did not want another fireman in the family so if you should find even one too many, I'll change. Keep smiling and remember everything comes to those who wait. Cheerio. Loving Brother Charlie

20 November 1944

All the kiddies will be getting grown up now and I look forward to seeing them all. Cheerio for now. All the best. Keep smiling Bert. Charlie xxx

It was good hearing about what people had been doing; whether or not half of it was true didn't matter. I felt better thinking that everything was carrying on as normal back home:

5 April 1942

It's nice to know you all go to dances and I wish I were able to. (But I cannot dance). Cheerio for now. Your loving Brother Charlie xxxx

21 September 1942

Have you a tandem also or do you ride a scooter. Thank Marjorie for her letter. I hope you all receive letters from me. Loving Brother Charlie xxx

But what was I meant to write? What news could I tell them? 'Today I shared a bath with Sid and got an extra slice of bread.' Or 'Hurt my hand yesterday, breaking up rocks in the quarry.' I certainly couldn't have told them 'Watched a man being beaten to death today'. I didn't tell them about such things then, nor after the war.

As far as other communications went, we had postcards we could send – not quite 'Wish you were here' ones from the seaside. They were camp photographs which had been made into postcards. This was standard practice in POW camps, part of the ongoing German propaganda campaign and went on throughout the war. They were a way of showing everybody at home how well the Germans were treating their prisoners – all those rows of young men, smiling at the camera, trying to say 'Cheese'.

I don't think my family received any of the cards but some survived my journey home. The back of one photograph came in handy, as did the inside pages of my New Testament, to make notes about the things I saw and did on The March. I thought that if I didn't survive maybe somebody would find the card and know what we had gone through. *Postcard from Hell,* that's what it was, I'm afraid, when I read it now:

[March 30]

Two more of our men have passed away. We're badly in need of food, a bath & clothing. Sid collapsed at work and also others. The guards are inhuman.

[31 March]

Yanks billet bombed.

I am glad this one didn't get home to my mother.

When I look at the photograph now, I think it was remarkable how clean and tidy we all look, considering what we were going through. We must have made quite a bit of effort to get ourselves looking half-way decent. Rows of us standing at ease or sitting cross legged like children posing for a school photograph. Everybody is looking straight at the camera, putting on a good show for the folks back home. The photographs were taken at the back of the house we were living in, some time in 1941, I think. It looks as though we are sitting in somebody's back garden, not like a prison camp. They couldn't get us all in one photo so we were split up but my four pals are together with me on this one picture.

There's me in the back row with what people call my cheeky grin, probably because I am next to Jimmy who has made a joke about something and made me laugh. I am wearing my non-regulation cap that was made for me by my tailor friend. There is Sid, in the middle row, and Laurie, in the front row, with Heb who doesn't look at all well. We didn't know that Hebby had a heart condition and he collapsed on The Long March home. He survived and I saw him once after the war but he died in 1960. And there is a chap named Sargent; you could always see the marks on his tunic where his three stripes had been. So he was actually Sergeant Sargent. You can't forget that, can you?

I remember it was a few days before we were liberated by the Americans, after our four months on the road, one of the guards was walking down the column of men and struck Sergeant Sargent across the face with the butt of his rifle. There was blood everywhere and Sargent's nose was broken. Later an American soldier saw the injury and asked Sargent what had happened. When he told him, the American asked if he could identify the guard and Sargent said he could. He was taken to a huge compound where the German soldiers were being held and he was able to identify the man who was then taken away and shot, so I believe. We all felt that justice had been done. The guard got what he deserved.

It was a Polish lad, about sixteen, who came and took our pictures. He was from the Home nearby and was ordered to do the job by the *Unteroffizier.* I think it must have been on a Sunday, our day off. When he had finished taking the photos, he left us and we never saw him again. The last we heard, three or four days' later, was that he had been arrested and sent to a concentration camp.

The Home he was staying at was a sort of hostel for young Polish workers which had been built in a field not far from us. We watched the foundations being laid as we passed on our way to work each day, and then the brick walls rising over the next few months. What the Germans did every now and then was to go down a street in the early hours of the morning, knocking on all the doors, and if there were families with children, they would take away all the youngsters, mostly aged 14 to 16 or 17 years (old enough to work). They sent them to these homes all over the region where they stayed and were sent out to work, like us, on neighbouring farms. Extra labour was needed all the time to keep up with the demand for food across the country.

The German authorities, who had built the Home near us, were not bothered about comfort so the building had only the most basic accommodation and facilities. There was no running water or electricity laid on so they used oil lamps. The boys had to collect fuel for the stoves and water from the bowsers or water tankers in the village about 5km away. The girls had domestic duties round the house. There were about 40 children looked after by an elderly Pole, at first, who wore a yellow arm band, and then a couple took over and the woman mainly supervised the girls. It was upsetting to think of those children being in a similar position to us. They were forced to work in the house as well as slaving away on the land and separated from their loved ones. We used to see the boys and girls out on the fields, bent over picking crops or carrying huge baskets of beet or potatoes but never near enough to talk to.

One day a group of us was working near the Home. We were weeding and clearing stones and debris on some land; back breaking work, getting it ready for ploughing. The guards were not around and we were able to stop and have a stretch and a ciggie every so often. I was standing looking at the view, acres and acres of emptiness, when I heard the sound of an engine in the distance. That high-pitched whining noise of an approaching motorbike. I saw a German policeman, in his funny helmet, come up the road and stop outside the building. He parked the motorbike and then walked up to the front door and knocked. He had to wait a minute or two before the woman in charge answered. He had a longish conversation with her on the step, showing her some papers or something, and then she went back inside.

A few minutes' later, she returned with a young girl, probably about 15 or 16 years old, holding her by the arm. The policeman grabbed the girl with both hands and marched her along the path, out to where his motorbike was standing. She was only a slight girl, wearing a flimsy floral dress and no coat, even though it was a chilly day. He slung her over the petrol tank at the front like a sack of potatoes, got on his bike and, holding her down with one hand, roared off down the road towards a little wooded area.

About ten minutes or so later, I heard the sound of the engine again and looked up. It was the same bike and policeman returning up the road. It stopped and the policeman got off, picked up the girl from the front and dumped her on the road outside the house. Poor thing, you wouldn't have recognised her from the state she was in. I swear he was laughing as he roared off again back the way he came.

And what had she done to deserve this brutal punishment? We heard later, that all she had tried to do was alter a *Brot-Karte* – bread card – she had got from one of the lads. She had scratched out a tick on it which showed that the allowance had already been taken. Hunger can drive you to do terrible things, I know, but that was nothing really, hardly what you call a crime. That policeman was wicked behaving like that – a law unto himself, just for his own sadistic pleasure.

Some Germans, the worst kind, laughed and joked while they carried out these attacks. I think they enjoyed it because it was a way of keeping everybody under their control, reminding them who was in charge. They showed you that they could do anything they liked. There was nothing to do but stand by and watch and hate them all the more. The longer the war went on, I felt that it might never end, that these awful things would go on forever and I might never see home again. There was no escape.

It wasn't any good dwelling on things like this too much. You would go mad if you did and some men did go crazy, not in our camp, thank heavens. We had to keep our spirits up and everybody tried to support each other if they could. No point in giving in or giving up. There was always somebody worse off than yourself.

When we weren't working, we enjoyed a smoke together, told jokes, and tried to entertain ourselves, all things which broke up the time and relieved the monotony. There was little opportunity to do anything else. Except, every month or so, there was an extra activity which the *Unteroffizier* offered us in exchange for cigarettes. However, I wasn't tempted to take on this particular one. I never did latrine duty.

This was important work, of course, and I am eternally grateful to those chaps who volunteered to do the job – clearing the pit out and transferring the contents to carts which were then taken off and dumped somewhere. Funnily enough, I never thought about where all our waste material went. Maybe it was part of the manure collected locally which we regularly spread on the fields. Maybe the potatoes we stole and brought back to cook and consume were ones grown in our own shit.

Our latrines were at the back of the house and consisted of a three-sided outhouse, about 20ft long, open at the front with a trench running the length. There was a pile of lime and a shovel at the side which you used to cover your evacuations. It didn't smell too bad as the lime seemed to do the trick of keeping it under control. We only used it during daylight hours as there was no lighting. Civilians came periodically in horse-drawn carts with loads of lime which they left for us. Every four to six weeks, a guard would come and ask for volunteers to clear out the latrines and replace the lime.

My only contribution to the hygiene of my fellow inmates was cutting up old newspapers into squares (when we managed to find any) which we strung together and then hung from the central pole which kept the roof on. Pity we never got an English newspaper, we could have read it first before wiping our backsides with it. Something to read would have been good, anything to stimulate our brains and give us another view of the outside world. Imagine yourself being cut off from the rest of the world with no telephones, newspapers, TV or radio and no transport to take you out somewhere different, to shop or visit a cinema. All we had was ourselves, our own thoughts and the company of other prisoners.

We liked the occasional sing song and tried our best to pick out songs which we all knew, like *Pack Up Your Troubles in Your Old Kit Bag* and *Bless 'em All*. Sadly, we were rather out of touch with the current music trends. We didn't know the latest songs by Vera Lynn or Anne Shelton that everybody was singing back home.

Jack, the musical one, once suggested that we put on a little concert. It was all a bit awkward as we didn't really know what to do and, like other people who were shy, I wouldn't have been able to stand up in front of everybody and perform even if I had any talent. We got started on it then dropped it because some bright spark said, 'Wouldn't it be better to do a play?' That didn't work either. I don't think we had anybody among us who was good enough to write a script or learn the lines.

What I really enjoyed was listening to people talking about themselves and what they did in civvy street. We had some spare rooms and one had a long table and some wooden forms in it, a bit like a schoolroom. We took some chairs from somewhere else so we could seat about twenty of us and we would sit and talk, each person giving a little talk for twenty minutes before moving on to the next one. It was interesting hearing about people's jobs and families and that's when I learned that a couple of fellows lived not far from me in Barking. We could spend whole evenings like this and sometimes it was the simplest, everyday things which fellows talked about that really held my attention. It made me yearn for the old days when life was simpler.

Another highlight of camp life was when there was delivery of new uniforms from the Red Cross. This didn't happen very often and I think the main camp had first pick from the look of what we landed up with. There were never enough clothes to go round so we had to wait our turn. I wore my original uniform for three years, that's the one I was wearing in the propaganda photographs. I took care of it all that time so that it lasted. I kept it clean, darned holes and reinforced seams. Some men didn't bother but it gave me something to do and gave me a sense of pride in keeping it going. After all, we were still British soldiers.

I was thrilled, of course, when I got something new. I remember a consignment of clothes arriving and it was my turn with Laurie to sit down to unpack them, sort them all out and check the sizes. They never had a full range of sizes, so it was pot luck getting a uniform which fitted. You weren't fussy. You thought yourself lucky to get something and most men were walking about in a mismatch of clothes. What did it matter? It wasn't a fashion parade.

I was a size 7 and ended up with size 16 trousers, much too big and long for me. So I cut the bottoms off, turned them inside out, gathered up the material and sewed them up to make a seam. Our tailor chap was a wizard with offcuts, so he snapped them up for future use, showing us how to make mittens (like little pockets for your hands) also using strips cut off our blankets. They came in handy when we working in very cold, wet weather and they were also easy to dry, unlike your clothes. Pop your mittens under your straw mattress or pillow and the warmth would dry them out.

It's funny thinking about it now, how excited we got over the simplest everyday thing. A pair of new socks, an extra slice of sausage, a game of football, a letter from home, a dry coat, a boiled sweet, a sunny day, a guard who looked the other way. But, you know, I think life was the same for a lot of people at that time. Nothing was normal. You could take nothing for granted any longer. At home there was rationing and shortages, the fear of bombing and of receiving a letter from The War Office through your letter box.

Fear ruled everybody's life. The local people were afraid of the authorities and not complying with orders, fearing reprisals if they didn't do as they were told. They saw their farms and land taken over and their children sent away. They didn't like to be seen speaking to us or showing us any favours. We would love to have got to know some of the people we worked alongside or indeed help them.

Several times we were called to unload the coal wagons at the railway station. This was winter fuel for the villagers and we spent a couple of days shovelling it from the wagons into carts, which then went off to storage places nearby. We got really filthy dirty doing this. Imagine standing by the open side of the wagon as the coal all comes hurtling down as soon as you dig into the pile. Never mind, we knew the locals appreciated what we did, even if they couldn't say anything to us. A smile was enough.

Now there were always little bits of coal at the bottom of the wagon and some of the elderly people, usually women, from the village would bring baskets and crawl under the trucks to pick up any bits which had fallen through the gaps onto the line. So what we did when we were down to the last bit of the load was to find a decent hole in the floor of the wagon and push nuggets of coal through for the women underneath to pick up. We were not doing any harm to the Germans or costing them anything; we were just helping these old people get a bit of extra fuel for their stoves. And winters there were long and hard, bitterly cold with the snow and ice lasting six months or more.

Many of these elderly folk were struggling to keep going in their own homes. Families had been broken up, sons and grandsons had left, conscripted or taken away forcibly. If a man in our country did not want to go to war he could be a conscientious objector and do other work, such as going down the mines or serving in the medical corps. But in Germany they couldn't refuse to fight or they and all their family could be sent to a concentration camp.

Our guards turned a blind eye to a bit of coal pilfering. They were quite privileged away from front line. It may have been boring for them and they didn't have many luxuries either, but they were pretty safe. As long as they obeyed orders, said '*Heil, Hitler*' to the officers and didn't get caught with a tin of Player's cigarettes, they were all right. It was a break for them, to be sent out there to guard us for a couple of months before being sent back to the fighting.

So everybody tried to keep things on an even keel. None of us prisoners wanted to step out of line as it could have repercussions for everybody else. The guards didn't want any trouble as that could reflect badly on them and they wanted so stay on at the camp because they were out of harm's way. So we put up with things. But sometimes, once in a while, it didn't take much to tip you over the edge.

9

Not Fit for Pigs

Every day started and ended the same: thinking about food from the moment you got up to when your head hit the straw mattress at night. You were looking forward to each meal, whatever you were given, hoping there might be something different or a little bit more. Mug of coffee for breakfast, thin, greasy soup for lunch, and a piece of bread and butter and a slice of bratwurst, if you were lucky, for supper. Play cards. Darn your socks. Write a letter. Go to bed hungry. Always the same.

Except that day. I will always remember that particular day as one thing distinguished it from all the thousands of other days spent in exactly the same way.

Mid July. Warm and dry. It was harvest time. That day I was in a different working party. There were eleven of us, including pals Laurie and Jimmy, and we were working on a small farm helping the farmer, his wife and their daughter with the harvest. We were in a hay barn and we were moving sheaves of wheat with pitch forks from one side of a huge barn to the opposite bay. We were giving the hay a good airing so it didn't rot or get eaten by vermin. I was up top with three others, throwing the sheaves down to the five below, who passed them to the other three in the empty bay. It was hard work and it was hot, and the dust from the wheat got in the back of my throat. We had rolled up our sleeves and tied string round the bottom of our trousers to stop the mice getting up our legs when their nests were disturbed in the wheat. They ran out, babies and adults, all over the place, looking for another safe place to settle.

Good old Jimmy had come prepared. He usually carried an assortment of useful things in his pockets including string which he saved from the Red Cross Parcels. Just the ticket. It was funny though, because you wouldn't think to look at it that the string was actually made out of brown paper. It was all twisted very, very tightly but if you unravelled it, you would see what it was made of. Of course, it was no good in the rain as it just fell to bits. It was hot and sweaty work but still better than freezing to death in the middle of a field in winter, hacking at sugar beet in the frozen ground with a useless two-pronged hand tool.

A guard came across the farm yard. It was lunch time. You could hear the sound of the hooves and the wheels of the cart on the cobbles coming towards us with our food. The sound of the metal ladle like a reveille, clanking on the milk churn full of soup. I heard a voice shouting something in German, probably, '*Los!*' – get going, or '*Schnell, schnell!*' – hurry up, to the camp cooks or maybe to us. We stopped work, put down our tools and made our way out of the barn. I wiped my hands on my trousers as I followed the others. As I came round the side of the barn, I could see our chaps struggling to keep the churn upright on the back of the cart.

Soup of the day. Glorious soup of the Fatherland! Soup was all we usually had at midday after a long, hard morning's work. Hot and wet, maybe a surprise bit of meat or lump of swede, a scrap of beet leaf, but nothing much to recommend it. I couldn't see anything else on the cart. No bread. No such luck. If you were clever enough, or rather strong enough, you saved a piece from the night before to have with your soup the next day but most of the time you didn't. It took an iron will not to wolf it down as soon as you got your evening ration.

We always carried our bowls and spoons with us so I went and collected mine where I had left them in the large inside pocket of my overcoat, which was hanging on a post. I went and queued at the cart where one of our chaps was standing ready, ladle in hand. You would have thought it was precious liquid gold the way he was serving it out, taking his time, careful not to spill a drop as the ladle travelled the distance between churn and bowl. 'Come on, come on. I'm hungry,' I said.

It was my turn and I held my bowl out with my hand cupped underneath to keep it steady. Didn't want to lose a drop. Maybe it was special that, I was thinking. Perhaps one of the camp cooks had added a bit of something extra. As it was served out into my bowl, I could feel that the soup was stone cold and I thought that this was rubbish. This was no good. I tipped the bowl forward slightly to look inside and gave the soup a sniff. Terrible. What on earth was in it? Bits of rancid horse meat in a scummy grey liquid. How could anybody serve something like that to another human being? How were you meant to work twelve hours a day on this pig swill?

Now I had a terrible temper, I admit that, and something just went inside me sometimes. I lost all sense of where I was and what was going on around me. I didn't care that the chap who made the soup was looking at me, worried that I was going to say something. That the fellow before me had already drunk his down in one go. I didn't care who was standing next to me, behind me or across the yard. I was angry, so angry that I couldn't stop myself. I walked over to the guard. I didn't even take in which one it was. I did not care who it was. They were all the same that day.

We had a number of guards who came and went all the time. You marched out in the morning with one lot and by then end of the day there had been two or three changes. There was Hunchback Hans, the one I gave cigarettes to in exchange for a bit of extra bread; Red Face who loved garlic; or the ones we nicknamed Taffy Biscuits because they were all the same, only capable of shouting. '*Mach weiter. Mach weiter.*' – do more, do more, when we were working. You know – sounds like McVite, Mcvite's Biscuits, so Taffy Biscuits. Oh, never mind. And there was Jan who didn't like the English and me in particular.

So this lunchtime guard was sitting on a wall, his rifle propped up next to him, head down, chewing and sucking his teeth. I walked across to him.

'Look,' I said, shoving the bowl under his nose, stabbing my finger at the disgusting mess in it. 'That's not fit for pigs,' adding, '*Für Schweine*,' – for pigs, in case he didn't understand. Then I repeated the word, '*Schweine!* ' and threw the contents of the bowl across the yard. The soup sort of curved up in the air for a second before it landed, splattering across the cobbles, leaving a greasy stain and then seeped away through the cracks. OK, that was done, I had made my point. I imagined that the guard was saying to himself, 'If you don't want it, then that's your loss. You don't eat it, you go hungry.' End of story.

So I turned and walked off towards the stables where they kept the farm horses. There was a tap outside where you washed your hands, cleaned your bowl and sneaked a drink if you were lucky. I was bending down to turn on the tap and rinse out my bowl when I heard the guard get up. Now German soldiers wore boots with steel toe caps and heels and I heard the clack, clack sound of his boots on the cobbles coming towards me. Oh God, he was following me.

I straightened up and turned round to face him. It was Jan, it would be, the guard who didn't like me. He was a very big bloke, over 6 ft tall. He was what was known as *einer falsche Deutscher* – a false German, half Polish, neither one thing nor the other, I suppose. He had never liked me. Not that I had ever done anything in particular to him. I was English, a prisoner of war and he didn't like the look of my face. He was coming straight at me now, fixing his bayonet to his rifle, which should have been fixed all the time by their law. He speeded up and when it was finally attached he suddenly lunged at me and caught me in the chest with the bayonet. I felt a sharp pain, which spread across my chest and made me gasp.

He wasn't trying to spear me, I didn't think, just give me a bit of scare. I dodged out of the way as I saw another one coming but the tip caught me in the side in the rib cage. That hurt too. I was unlucky; not quick enough. So when I saw a third one coming my way, I'd had enough. I grabbed his rifle by the barrel and with tremendous force pulled it out of his hand and threw it on the ground. It was a bloody stupid thing to do as there was bound to be a round of ammunition in the gun. I knew it because their rifles were meant to be loaded at all times. It might have triggered off and killed either one of us or one of my friends. What a stupid thing to do! Me and my temper. If I had killed a German guard that would have been certain death.

My two pals ran to me and got between me and Jan. Jimmy was shouting at me, pretending to tell me off, and Laurie was holding me off with one hand and waving the other at Jan as though to say, 'It's OK, OK, I've got him.' Jan looked as though he had had enough. He was thinking, 'I've given him a fright, shown him who's in charge, and his mates have got him now and are telling him off.' I took deep breaths and then let go and felt Jimmy and Laurie holding me, taking control.

Another guard arrived to take over from Jan. Jimmy and Laurie marched me away and told me what a bloody idiot I was. They were cross and said, 'You could have got yourself killed.' I looked over my shoulder and saw that Jan had retrieved his rifle and was checking the bayonet. I saw from his face and gestures that he was telling guard No 2 about what had happened. Telling him all about me and what I had done to the soup and to him. He disappeared and we went back to the hay barn to finish the job.

It was painful trying to work, especially bending down and stretching up. My chest and ribs hurt and my shoulder felt as though it was coming out of its socket. I opened my tunic a little and rubbed the area through my vest. It was sore. There was bruising; it would be purple by morning. I carried on working, well, going through the motions. Afternoon turned into evening. There was another change of guard and we finished about seven and marched back to our camp.

Nobody said anything on the way home but we all returned in a good mood, looking forward to something to eat, especially me. Anything to take the edge off the awful hunger. No breakfast and my lunch left on the ground in the farmyard so I hoped that there was a bit of *Wurst* that night.

Word had got round about the incident, presumably from our cooks and as I entered the camp yard, some of the chaps who had returned earlier called out, 'All right, Tyro, what you been up to, then?' Some of the chaps used that nickname. Apparently Tyro was an Indian word for 'Wait' and I suppose I got it, not just because of my surname but because I had been known to get a bit impatient over things. One of the cooks joined in: 'Fancy some soup, then, or shall I cut out the middle man and chuck it straight on the floor?' They knew about the trouble with the guard and wanted to know more.

'Go on, Tyro, what you do?' But we were interrupted by the *Unteroffizier* calling us all to order. Everybody was told to go inside except me. '*Hier bleiben,'* – stay here, he said. What was this? I was thinking. This looked like trouble. I was worried then because Jan had obviously reported me or word had got back to the *Unteroffizier* from the other guard. I didn't know what was going to happen next. They were not going to forget it. I was going to be charged, wasn't I? Charged and punished.

The officer said, *'Name und Nummer,'* – give me your name and number, which I did. 'Private Charles Waite Number 10511,' and added '*Mein Herr.*' He handed me a postcard on which was typed in English 'POW Charles Waite No 10511 is to be taken to the *Kommandant* at Headquarters under arrest on a charge of Incitement to Mutiny.' Mutiny! I couldn't believe it. That frightened the life out of me. My heart was pounding and I could hardly breathe. I felt as though I was going to faint because I knew, I knew what the penalty was for such a serious charge.

Mutiny. In Germany in the First World War that meant a man could be shot so there was no reason for this lot to behave any differently. I was scared to death. I thought of my mother and of Lily, how upset they would be. All the family.

The officer said, '*Komm hier früh,'* – be here early, '*um sechs Uhr morgens,'* – at six o'clock in the morning. He walked off sharply and I was left standing there alone. When I went in and told the others, my pals tried to reassure me, 'Don't worry, Chas. You'll be back.' And 'You haven't hurt anyone. It's just to put the wind up you. Don't worry about it.' But I was worried, very worried. Incitement to Mutiny. Headquarters. *Kommandant.* You couldn't forget that.

I couldn't get to sleep for thinking about it. I lay awake in my bunk listening to the strange noises in the night and worrying. Oh, God, spare me, I prayed. I was up well before the time and everybody wished me good luck. 'See you later, Chas,' and 'Chin up, Tyro.' I went and waited by the main entrance for the guard and it was Jan who was going to escort me to HQ.

We set off walking towards Freystadt and arrived at the station about half an hour later, where a train was waiting. It was just an engine and two carriages and we headed for the first one. Nobody else was allowed on and I saw people – civilians, being directed to the rear carriage. A guard shouted, '*Hier nicht,*' – not here, and pointed saying, '*Im hinteren Wagen*' – the rear carriage. When I got inside I went to sit down but Jan indicated with his rifle for me to get up. I stood at the back while Jan made himself comfortable on a seat in the middle of the empty carriage.

After about twenty minutes, the train stopped and we got off and went on another train with a single carriage. When we arrived at our destination, about an hour later, we had to climb down and cross the railway tracks to get to the main road. It was empty countryside for miles around. No signs or landmarks. We didn't talk or communicate in any way as we walked side by side, a short distance apart. All the time I was frightened, thinking about the charge, where we were going and what was going to happen.

Suddenly we came to a sharp bend and as we rounded it the barracks appeared ahead. The battalion headquarters were massive, thousands of German troops were stationed there. There was a field to the left with half a dozen small planes, which looked like observation aircraft. Jan led the way, marching smartly now, as we approached the main gates where two guards outside checked our papers, and opened the gates. As soon as we were through and standing in a small square, they locked the gates and we walked towards another set of gates. Two more guards repeated the palaver and we went through the gates into a larger square with buildings all around. I had no idea where I was. I didn't recognise anything. I wondered if I would ever get out of there, back to my pals at the camp.

Jan asked a guard something, probably where the guardhouse was, and the guard pointed across the way. The place was noisy and busy with people coming and going. As I stood there, I felt very small and very afraid. I was nothing. Nobody. Off we went again with Jan pushing me forward to the entrance to a building and up some wooden steps. We went along a corridor and up more steps into a huge hall with high ceilings and a beautiful polished floor. There wasn't any furniture in the room and I felt even more afraid in these surroundings. Still not saying a word to me, Jan pushed me against a wall, and I stood to attention automatically.

At the far end was an enormous framed picture of Hitler, his eyes staring straight at me. Behind me was Göring. I could just see his face over my shoulder if I turned my head slightly and that made me feel even more nervous. Who was going to come out of the door the other side and along that corridor? I would be going through there any minute. Somebody was going to come out and call my name. Me, all on my own in this place. I could have done with a friend right then. I was wondering if I would see Laurie and Jimmy or Sid and Heb again. Had they finished work and were having lunch? Soup again, no doubt. Maybe they were having a crafty smoke behind the stables.

It felt a long time standing to attention but it was probably about five minutes when Jan decided he had had enough. He was standing to the side of me, his rifle propped up against the wall. Now I had the feeling all along that Jan was a bit of an idiot. Fancy leaving your rifle propped up when guarding a prisoner for a start – and in a place like this. He walked round the front of me and said, '*Bleiben hier. Ja.*' – stay here, yes. I understood and replied '*Ja*'. He walked off and away down the steps and disappeared. I could hear voices and he was asking somebody about a drink – '*Zu trinken*,' and if there was a canteen – '*Wo ist die Kantine*? He didn't come back so I just remained standing there on my own waiting for something to happen.

Suddenly two German officers appeared from the other end and they walked towards the opening where their offices were, I imagined. Those boots again, with those steel tips and heels, which went clack, clack, clacking across the polished wooden floor. To give them due, they were the smartest looking officers, and their uniforms were way above anything I had ever seen. Immaculate, everything beautifully polished and starched. They really were just the ticket. One was wearing the Iron Cross on a ribbon round his neck, and there wasn't a crease in his uniform. They disappeared for a little while and then I heard the boots again. They came back and one said something to the other one.

Oh, God, what was that? Iron Cross came over to speak to me and I was taken aback. He said in absolutely perfect English. 'Who are you and what are you doing here?' and I thought, Thank God, an English man! You could always tell a German trying to speak English by their pronunciation of *zee* instead of *th* as in *the;* but there was no trace of that. It was laughable. I was so relieved and then immediately felt frightened again. If he was English and turned German I was in serious trouble. He could be really hostile to any fellow Englishman if he had turned against his own country. If they were going to try me then things could get much worse for me.

'Where is the guard?'

'I don't know, sir.'

'Has he gone to the office?'

'No, sir.'

'Has he gone out?'

So I said, 'Yes, sir.' I told him the truth. 'He went out.'

So Iron Cross went to the far end, opened the door and called out, '*Gehen und ihn!*' – go and get him.

I was watching all this going on when I saw Jan come back in. The silly idiot came up the steps, pushed the door open, entered and stood beside me. He didn't look over the other side where the two officers were standing right under Hitler. When he finally looked up and across, he saw them, grabbed his rifle and stood to attention. What else could he do? The officers crossed the floor again towards him. Jan stood to attention and they all exchanged '*Heil Hitler*'. Iron Cross gave him a terrible dressing down. You didn't need to speak German to understand what he said. And then they went off back inside and we were left standing there again.

I thought that had helped me a bit; he was in trouble and that might make it easier for me when they came to deal with me. But then I found out that they were nothing to do with me, too high-ranking to be hearing a case like mine.

Clack, clack, more heels, but female ones this time, and a woman in civilian clothes appeared and said something to the guard in German. Jan grabbed hold of my epaulette and started pulling me along as he followed the woman down the corridor. She entered the room first and my guard pushed me inside and disappeared.

There were two officers sitting behind a large desk. One looked like a 2nd Lieutenant and the other a Sergeant Major, *Hauptfeldwebel.* At the far end of the room at another table sat a uniformed woman tapping away on one of those large sit-up-and-beg manual typewriters. One asked me my name again '*Name und Nummer*' and I said it again. The civilian woman looked on silently. I thought she was probably from the Red Cross and if this was my trial then she was here as a neutral observer to see that things were done correctly. I wished she would say something to me; a word of comfort wouldn't have gone amiss. The other officer asked me my name and number again and pushed a foolscap sheet of paper across the table to me along with a pen. I was trembling and my palms were sweating. What was this? Didn't I get the chance to speak? I bent down to pick the pen up and I looked at the paper. Of course it was all in German. No idea what it said. So I put the pen down and pushed the piece of paper back to him.

'*Ich verstehe nicht.*' – I don't understand, I said.

'Egal, ' – doesn't matter, was the reply and he pushed the paper back to me.

I pushed it away again. '*Ich verstehe nicht.*' As scared as I was, I was not going to sign that piece of paper. I could have been signing my death warrant for all I knew. So I didn't sign and left it on the table and stood to attention.

The officers looked at each other and started talking; they consulted Red Cross Lady who nodded and left the room. A moment later, she returned with a middle-aged chap in uniform who told me, in broken English, that he had been a prisoner of war in England at the end of the last war. So with his bit of English and my bit of German I learned that the charge of 'Incitement to Mutiny' had been dropped and changed to a lesser one of 'Sabotage, wasting food and damaging army property'. I was so relieved that I nearly cried with relief. Although I was still frightened about what would happen next.

My guard was called back in and off we went again. Jan was still pulling me by my epaulette, taking the same way back. Across the squares, through the gates, on to the road to the station, on to a train, and so on, back to camp. It was dark when I got in and my pals were there, pleased to see me.

Jimmy patted me on the back and said something like, 'A wee break like that does you the world o' good.' Sid gave me bit of bread and butter that he had kept back from supper. Laurie lit me up a cigarette and Heb said, 'Good to see you in one piece.'

And that was it. I didn't hear any more about it. It sort of fizzled out. I got away with it, or so I thought.

A week passed before I heard anything more; I really thought they had forgotten about it. Jan was still around on duty but he never came out on any job I was on. It was Friday after work and the guards had got us lined up outside. The *Unteroffizier* arrived and called out my name again. I stepped forward. He held two cards and handed me one typed in English and read out the other in German. I was to be taken to Stalag 20B to do ten days' solitary confinement. And I was scared all over again.

I went to collect my things, my greatcoat and bundle. My pals rallied round. 'Don't worry, could have been worse,' and collected what biscuits they had saved from their last Red Cross parcels. 'You'll be all right.' I had three or four biscuits of my own and they added some more until I had about a dozen in the end, wrapped in a scrap of paper. A real feast. 'Got to save 'em. Don't know when you'll eat again,' they said to me.

Two guards escorted me this time, a similar route it seemed, except we were going to the main camp at Marienburg. You never knew where you were half the time. There were so many camps and forts which formed the overall Stalag 20B and there were prisoners coming and going out on work detachments all over the area. There were few signs or landmarks to get a sense of place. Any names I saw meant very little to me in relation to anywhere else.

I was standing on my own again in a train, the two guards sitting together in the middle. One took out a packet from inside his jacket, unwrapped it and started to eat. It looked to me as though he'd got a boiled egg and some bread and butter. Oh well, I thought, I'll eat something too as I missed breakfast. I bent down and put my hand inside my kit bag and felt for the paper packet of biscuits and managed to draw one out.

'*Essen verboten!*' – no eating, the guard shouted and I jumped and nearly dropped my bit of food. He got back to eating and I put the biscuit in a pocket. It was going to get all smashed up which was a shame. It would just be crumbs by the time I got there. So I stood and watched the guard munching, and the empty countryside going by while thinking about my biscuits.

The main camp was in the middle of the town surrounded by high walls and barbed wire. I looked up at one of the watchtowers as we went through the main gates. We had the usual ritual of checking papers, opening and closing gates. The guards took me across a square, up some wooden steps into a building and down some dark and dismal corridors. No idea where I was or what was ahead. One of them opened a door, pushed me in and shut the door behind me.

There was an assortment of different furniture. A chair, made up of odd bits of wood nailed together, one of those folding card tables with a rather tatty green felt top and a wall cupboard, locked with a padlock. There was a single iron bed with a palliasse and three folded blankets on it. I prodded the straw mattress which rustled nicely and felt and smelt freshly filled. Not bad. I felt the blankets, and I gave them a sniff too. Quite clean and not too rough.

'This isn't too bad. I could stick this for ten days,' I said to myself. Better settle in, so I took off my overcoat and laid it on the bed; put my bundle, which contained my bowl and spoon, toothbrush, piece of rag, which acted as a flannel, on the table and sat down and waited to see what would happen next.

10

Birthday Party

'What the bloody hell have you been doing to land up here?'

A British Army officer stood in the doorway shouting at me. I jumped up and stood to attention. I did know that much, even though I hadn't saluted anybody since being captured. I was too shocked to speak. I didn't like the sound of this. Why was he shouting at me?

'All right, Private, at ease. You can sit down,' he said. 'What's been going on then to land up here?' So I told him everything that had happened, leading up to that point.

'Bloody stupid, eh? Could have got yourself shot.'

'Yes, sir,' I said. I didn't need him to remind me.

'You're here now, still in one piece. Right. We'll have to see what's what, won't we?' He went over to the cupboard, undid the padlock, opened the door and took out a stethoscope.

What an idiot I was! Of course, he was the camp doctor come to check me over before I started my sentence. Then I knew that this was his cupboard, his table and his bed. If this was his room where was I going to be sleeping?

'So, do you think you can do this?' asked the doctor as he unravelled the stethoscope.

I wasn't sure what he meant. My last medical had been on my call up. I was classified 'A' then, I was probably 'Z' now.

'Take your shirt off, man. Do you think you can take the solitary?'

I started to undo the buttons of my tunic but my fingers didn't seem to work properly and I fumbled with them. Do solitary? Was I fit enough? You can't say no, can you? Can't be a whinger. I was as fit as any man, I thought, who'd been in a POW camp for years, forced to work outside all year, come rain or shine, twelve hours a day, six days a week. I took a deep breath and said, 'Yes. I can do it.' I still didn't know what was going to happen to me.

The doctor listened to my chest and did the same to my back. 'Deep breaths. Cough. OK.' He looked into my eyes and mouth and checked my pulse. He told me to put my shirt back on and he returned his stethoscope to the little cupboard. 'Not in bad shape considering. You're going to be on half rations, you know. Think you can make it?' I nodded. Half of nothing much, thinking of what we normally got.

'Now you know talking isn't allowed. Mustn't speak, not to anyone. Not even the guards, all the time you're in here. Or in the yard when you exercise or when you have a wash. Keep your mouth shut.' His eyes caught sight of my bundle. 'What've you got in there?'

'Just the usual, sir. Washing things. Bowl and spoon.' I opened it up to show him and he peered inside.

'What's that?' The doctor pointed at my little pack of biscuits and started to fold back the paper to have a look. 'Right, you got biscuits. You can't take them in. Not allowed to take in any food. Didn't they tell you?'

I didn't think he wanted me to reply or to hear that nobody had told me anything. I continued standing in silence, watching him as he took out my precious biscuits and stacked them neatly in a pile on a shelf in his cupboard.

That's a shame, I thought, they would have come in handy. No breakfast that day and only a meagre piece of bread and bit of sausage the previous night. I was dying for something to eat and drink. My heart sank when I heard the next statement.

'You should get a hot meal on the third or fourth day.'

'That's a long time to wait,' I thought. 'I haven't got any choice.' I was willing to bet though, that it would be soup.

'You can have some of these,' he said, and picked up some paperback books from the bottom shelf and handed them to me.

I would rather have my biscuits, I thought, but kept my mouth shut and slipped them into one of the inner pockets in my greatcoat.

The doctor looked me up and down one last time and patted me on the shoulder. I thought he was about to say, 'Chin up, young man, it'll be fine,' but all he did was open the door, put his head out and called for the guard.

A guard came in and gestured to me with his rifle. I picked up my coat and bundle and followed him, pausing for a moment before going out of the room. I looked at the doctor and the closed cupboard door where my biscuits were.

We walked along corridors and then passageways which got darker and colder and smellier. You wouldn't have known it was summer outside. We went down some steps and passed door after door. Then by the miserable light of a single bulb hanging down on a frayed cord, I could see one door ajar at the end. It had a tiny pane of frosted glass high up with barbed wire tacked outside. The guard kicked the door open, pushed me in and then slammed the door shut behind me.

It was almost completely dark inside so I couldn't make out a thing. I felt my way around until my foot hit something and I tripped and fell. It was some sort of board fixed to the wall. Ah, that was my bed. I patted my way along it till I felt a rough blanket. What a stink! Better off without it. I wasn't going to sleep under that so I pulled it off, dropped it on the floor and kicked it to the side. Well, it didn't have far to go. I suppose the cell was about 8ft by 8ft. I was to pace it out a few times A day over the next ten days.

What about a toilet? Now I wasn't used to anything fancy. Camp latrines are nothing to write home about and squatting down in a field is OK as long as you avoid nettles and thistles but what was I meant to do here? Were they going to let me out to go somewhere? A few seconds later I got my answer. Ting. I kicked something metallic in the corner, not a bucket but an empty jam tin, as it turned out. Germans like their jam and this tin was catering size and was empty at the start of my stay, thank goodness but very full by the end.

How long it was before I had any human contact I can't say. It was difficult keeping track of time in the dark like that and a watch wouldn't have helped much even if I'd had one. Sid was the only one with a watch, one which he had taken off a German soldier, I believe. I'm not sure under what circumstances but I wish he had thought of lending it to me anyway. I knew from what some of the chaps back at camp had said about the sentence that it wasn't just about being on your own but also having to survive on next to nothing to eat. We never had enough food as it was, so I knew I'd be having even less but the good thing was I wouldn't be out slaving away all day on the farm, coming back, worn out and starving. OK, ten days, yes, I can do that, I thought. Got to do it and put up with it. I kept thinking that this was nothing compared with what others had gone through or were even now experiencing.

I remembered what I had witnessed, what I had seen the Germans inflict on innocent people. My young army mates shot to bits in cross fire; the wounded soldiers on the makeshift operating tables; those poor Jews packed into cattle trucks, like us, but going to certain death; and that mother shot and her baby kicked like garbage down the railway track. There were prisoners dying of hunger and disease or sheer exhaustion all over the country. There were chaps who committed suicide because they couldn't take any more and just gave up. People on their own, with no pals like me. That was no way to be. Yes, I was lucky. I settled down, squatting on the board and sat there, waiting for the days to pass.

It was afternoon, I imagine, when I heard footsteps and the sound of boots kicking the doors along the corridor. This I learned was the signal for food or exercise or roll call. It was meal time. I found my bowl and got ready for the door to open. I knew it was going to be half rations but I was still surprised when I saw – or should I say felt, the tiny piece of bread, cube of butter and slice of liver sausage which had been chucked in the bowl by a rough and dirty hand. I had a glimpse of the face as well of the soldier in the half light of the doorway. I leaned later that it was Serb POWs doing a lot of the prison jobs.

So there I was, sitting alone in the dark in my overcoat, trying to make a meal out of my meagre rations. You always break your bread up into smaller pieces to make it go further. Use your spoon to smear the butter on each piece to give it a bit of taste. As for the *Wurst* you try to keep that till later. The pangs of hunger during the night or early morning were excruciating.

All of a sudden I heard a little bit of scuffling by the door. Oh God, not a rat! Is there nowhere safe from those horrible wretched creatures? We had them in the house and used to hear them gnawing through the floorboards at night. Like the sound of distant machine guns. Terrible! So we used to stamp on the floor to make them go away. But they always returned. At least I was off ground level there in an upper bunk. I thought I was meant to be doing solitary.

I was looking down at the bottom of the door where there was ¼ inch gap of light just about. It was a mouse. I saw its tail, a thin stringy affair not some great rope-like thing of a rat. It went back and forth a couple of times before disappearing. Then there was silence and all you could hear was me munching on my bit of bread.

A bit later the mouse came out again and it obviously knew there was food, probably smelt the liver sausage because it came out every night. Of course, it may have been a different mouse each time but I like to think that it was the same one keeping me company. So I broke off a tiny piece of bread, more a crumb really, and threw it towards the door. I waited and listened for the scurrying and then the movement of its tail in the pencil of pale light under the door. I'm sure I heard him nibbling away. My mouse, my Mickey Mouse.

On the fourth day, as I had been told, I was served my first hot meal – you've guessed it, soup. And this was about the worst I had ever had, worse than the soup that got me there in the first place. Yes, it was warm but it was made of sugar beet leaves and bits of rotten potatoes and smelt to high heaven. I doubt if even Mickey would have touched it if I had put it down for him. But I did drink it. Every last stinking drop.

And it was a day or two later, when I had counted out the days I had been in, I realised it must be about 23 July, Lily's birthday. So I thought I would have a little celebration, a party. Lily might not be here but she was still with me in my heart and as I couldn't celebrate with anybody else, I would share my meal with Mickey. When I got my food that evening, I broke off a tiny piece of bread again and this time, using the end of my spoon, cut off a tiny piece of the liver sausage to add as an extra treat. I put it down on the floor by the crack under the door. Then I sat on my bit of hard board and waited for Mickey to come out.

So there I was eating my meal while Mickey nibbled away on his. Happy Birthday, Lily, my sweetheart, so far away. Would I ever see you again? If I did would you still want to marry me? Perhaps, she had met someone else. Somebody who could dance. I was a different person now, especially the way I looked. I was never any great shakes in the looks department before the war but now, I thought, my mother wouldn't even recognise me and Lily would probably run a mile if she saw me. We were both twenty-two years old and I would have to wait another three years before I saw her again.

When Mickey had gone I was alone sitting in the dark, with just my thoughts for company. What was everybody else doing? I listened for signs of life beyond my cell. Nothing except the odd scuffling sound and noise of distant banging. What about my pals in the camp? Singing, laughing and playing cards. What about the ordinary people who were caught up in this dreadful war, trying to carry on as normal. The families, what was left of them, going about their business on the farms and in the surrounding villages while I sat there feeling sorry for myself. Cows were being milked, butter being made and washing hung out to dry.

It was sad that we weren't able to have any real contact with people outside the camp, perhaps to see a bit of their home life. We worked alongside the locals and shared a cigarette or two and accepted loaves of bread, but it was not enough to form a bond between us, like you would with a friend you see every day. What did they think of it all? There were Russian women prisoners who worked alongside us in the beet fields, backs bent, heads down. We never got the chance to exchange even a few words with them, only a smile or gesture maybe.

I remember once we were working near a lake towards the north of the region. There was a small community of people known as Kashubians living there. We were walking through their village and were close enough to hear them talking as we walked by – not German or Polish but a strange language. We tried to signal to them but the guards hurried over and pushed us on quickly. I would have loved to have spoken to them, or try to communicate, and have learned something about them and their lives. Perhaps if people talked more and fought less it would be a better world.

I had tried to think of things to do. Reading would be ideal, I thought, remembering that the doctor had given me some little paperback books. They were those Forces Special editions for POW camps on very thin paper with rather faint print. Now, it was a kind thought but how the devil was I going to read them? Everything was dark and, even though my eyes got used to it a bit, I still couldn't see anything really, certainly not the tiny print on the pages. I was crouched down trying to read one by the little bit of light coming from the bottom of the door. Impossible so I gave up and, I'm sorry to say, found a better use for some of the pages. Damaging army property again. Still the doctor meant well, I suppose.

It was very quiet most of the time except one night, I'd been in about three days and suddenly I was woken by loud footsteps down the corridor and this terrific racket of banging and shouting. It was the guards coming along kicking the cell doors and then calling out '*Bist du da?*' – are you there? How stupid! Where else would you be? You had to answer '*Ja*'. Apparently there'd been an escape but not from the prison. After I came out I learned that it had been down below, where the prisoners in the main camp had built a series of tunnels.

We were supposed to get regular breaks, to go out every morning for half an hour to exercise and get a quick wash in the wooden trough in the yard. I went out twice. Guards came and kicked the doors, opened them and shouted *'Heraus! Waschen'* – Out. Wash, and you grabbed your flannel and toothbrush and waited to be marched out to a small yard.

The other prisoners were a rough-looking lot but then this wasn't a holiday camp and I didn't know who they were or why they were there. You couldn't tell what nationality they were from their uniforms, which were more bits and pieces of odd clothing. There were English, French and Serbs, I think. And I didn't ask. I was very careful not to look up too much in case I caught someone's eyes and spoke by mistake. I didn't want the butt of a rifle between my shoulder blades. We took it in turns to wash our faces as best we could in the dirty water in the trough and then walk round and round the yard to stretch our legs and enjoy a tiny bit of sunshine on our faces.

Ten days isn't very long really. I mean, I wasn't being punished with hard labour or anything. That was what I was going back to. I wondered if the lads were thinking of me. Had they received any Red Cross parcels? Would they save some ciggies or jam for me? Were they right now boiling up some hot water to make a jelly from the rations? That would go down a treat right now.

Were there any letters waiting for me from Lily or sister, Winnie, and brother-in-law, Bert? What about my arch enemy, the guard, Jan, what was he up to? I felt sorry for him actually. He was a prisoner too of the same invading German Army. He would rather be at home, going to work at a local factory every day, having a laugh with his mates and going home to his wife and kiddies every night, and a meal of pork and dumplings laid out ready on the table, finished off with a tot of schnapps.

When I was eventually released, a guard came and fetched me and escorted me outside into the main camp. It felt good not being cooped up like I was, to look up and see a blue sky and breathe nice fresh air. To watch other people walking around outside. I might still be in a prisoner of war camp surrounded by high walls and barbed wire and watch towers but it was a relief to be out there with other men. We came down the steps and out through the gate and this chap was waiting, another English officer, and a prisoner of war, obviously.

'Right, now then. You're Private Charles Waite. Correct? 10511, your number?'

'Yes, that's right, sir.'

'Before we go any further, do you want to go back where you came from?'

'Yes, I do, sir.'

'Then, stay away from that main gate.' He pointed towards it. 'Because that's the town there.'

Funny that, if you stood in the right place you could see ordinary townsfolk passing by in the square. People free to go about their everyday business going to work and then home again.

'If they want somebody for work and you're standing there, they'll grab you and then that'll be it. Probably stay there. And you won't see your mates again back at your place.' He was like a school teacher telling a naughty pupil off. 'You wouldn't want that would you?'

I shook my head, 'No, I wouldn't.' I thought of Jimmy and Laurie, Sid and Hebby waiting for me to return. Jack and Bill and all the others.

'Because you'll always be there under their thumb, ready to go out to do their work, whatever it is. Never go near that corner up there. That wire's electrified. Keep away. Now you want something to eat I bet?'

'Yes, please. I've got some biscuits in a locker somewhere.' That's good, I thought. I'll get them back after all. I was starving.

'Forget the biscuits,' he said, 'You can take them back with you. We've put you in here.' He took me across the open square where a few prisoners were exercising and standing around smoking. There were rows of single-storey wooden huts and we went into one, turning into a small side room where there was a table, a couple of chairs and a single iron bed. Light was streaming in even though the panes of glass in the windows were greasy and dirty. It looked cosy and you could feel at home there but then I thought, I couldn't stay there, not have lived there permanently. I wouldn't have liked that, locked up behind those barbed wire and electric fences, along with the thousands of other men.

I was better off outside in the open, even if the work was hard. Work took your mind off what was going on or might happen. Yes, we saw terrible things happen which reminded us that war was never far away and that this what our men were fighting to stop. But we could get away from it, at least in our minds, when we were working.

There was nature all around us and we watched the seasons change on the farms. We walked out into vast, flat, open countryside, into those huge expanses of fields and pine forests. On the way we passed through hamlets and villages, with their stone built cottages and brick farm buildings. We heard church bells ring or horses hooves on cobbles. We had occasional glimpses of normal everyday life: women hanging out washing and children running around a yard. We had a different sort of freedom in my camp, I realised now. We didn't have guards breathing down our necks all the time when we were working. And we knew how to get out at night, if we wanted to, as long as we didn't do it too often. It didn't look as though you could ever get outside a camp like this.

'Would you like a shower first?'

'That'll be nice.' I hadn't had a proper wash for weeks before I went in. I was taken to a shower block which was a brick building with a row of cold water showers. Running water. Heaven, not having to share somebody else's filthy water. When I came back there was a meal waiting for me. On a battered tin plate was a fried egg sandwich, oozing fat and the yolk already running out from between two slices of bread. 'Where did you get this from?' I asked.

'Never you mind,' he said as I tucked in. I picked up the sandwich and crammed it into my mouth, nearly choking with excitement and hunger. I licked my fingers (and the plate) to make sure every last bit had gone. That egg tasted so good. The last one I'd had must have been several months before, probably one that Jimmy had sneaked into the camp.

I found out afterwards that the officer was on the escape committee and that was why he knew so much about me and wasn't going to have any nonsense from me. He didn't want any trouble which could draw attention to what had been going on underground with their escape tunnels. To think that I could well have been sitting right on top of one of them; with men burrowing beneath my cell floor while I was sitting there twiddling my thumbs, dreaming of a bowl of mutton stew and dumplings.

It was lucky in a way that I got punished for my 'Insubordination' because it gave me the chance to see what was going on elsewhere and meet these other fellows in the camp. I stayed the night, bunking up with some of the lads and we had a laugh and swapped stories. It was good to hear a bit of news about what was happening in the war. You felt so cut off and not part of anything connected to what we had been called up for back in October 1939. Obviously they had access to a radio from the things they were telling me about this invasion and that attack. I learned more about what was happening to the Poles and Jews and their families and heard about what was happening in the concentration camps. I thought about Stutthof, the place not far from us.

In the morning I waited outside for my guard who was going to escort me back to camp. I kept well away from the main gate and perimeter fence as I watched men with sunken eyes, pale skin and skinny arms and legs walk by. I don't suppose I looked any better than them although my face and arms were quite brown from spending so much time out of doors. And although I was thin, I was fit with muscles in places I never knew you had them. Yes, I had something to be thankful for. I had remained pretty healthy with no serious illnesses and I see now how that was a good preparation for what came later – The Long March home. But I had another two years to wait for that.

My guard arrived and I was about to leave when someone came up behind me and tapped me on the shoulder. 'Yours, I believe,' and handed me with my little packet of biscuits.

When I returned to my camp I was welcomed back by everybody who crowded round, patted me on the back and gave me a cigarette. 'All right, Chas,' and 'Good to see you, mate,' and 'Saved you a bit of bacon.' I felt like a returning hero even though I had done nothing brave except sit out my solitary in a dark cell. I vowed never to do anything stupid like that again. 'Yeah, that's right, Chas. You keep your nose clean.'

I was careful after that because I was frightened of being punished again, of possibly going to a place called Graudenz where serious offenders were sent. We had heard stories from men we met from other work detachments, about what went on there. 'You don't want to go to that hell hole,' they said. 'Dreadful place. You go in for a month, do 12 hours a day unloading bricks, sand and cement from the barges. Live on half rations, return to your own camp for a couple of days to recuperate and then go back again.' Absolute torture.

When I think of it now, I was lucky; I got off lightly. Unfortunately having a bit of a temper is part of my character and not something so easily controlled when, in the heat of the moment, you think something is wrong or you witness an injustice, it's hard to keep quiet and do nothing. The soup incident was pretty mild compared with what I foolishly did a few months later.

11

A Nice Bit of Cheese

There's nothing worse than toothache once it starts and if you can't get any relief, it drives you crazy. One of our chaps did it himself, took out his own tooth with a penknife. Now I didn't fancy doing that, not just because of the pain but the sight of blood all over the place. My toothache went on for days and I couldn't eat or sleep properly. Eventually I couldn't stand it any longer.

I went to see the *Unteroffizier* in his office to ask him if I could go and see a dentist. He was sitting at a desk and stamping bits of paper, moving them from one pile to the next as Hitler looked down on him from the wall behind. I waited for him to finish what he was doing. I realised that I didn't know the word for dentist. Or tooth. Never mind, you just have to have a go, don't you. One of my big regrets is that I didn't learn German while I was in the camp. We picked up odd words and repeated phrases we heard but it was very limited; we never had proper conversations. If we had been allowed to speak more to the guards it would have been good.

When he finally looked up I said, '*Entschuldigen Sie. Ich brauche einen Dentist bitte,*' – Excuse me. I need a dentist, please, and pointed inside my mouth and pulled a face as if in pain, which, of course, I was. 'Tooth hurts. Tooth *schlecht*,' – bad.

'*Zahnartz, ja*?' he said.

'*Ja,*' I said, nodding. '*Ich brauche einen Zahnartz, bitte*.'

'*Nein. Kein Zahnartz*.' – no, no dentist. He shook his head and dismissed me with a wave, adding, '*Keine Zeit. Keine Soldaten,*' – no time, no guards.

He couldn't spare one of his men just to take one prisoner all the way into town to a dentist and then back again. And that was that.

The toothache continued and I was just considering borrowing a penknife and having a go myself when Laurie and Sid came up with an idea.

'Oh, Chas, my tooth hurts,' said Laurie, pulling a face.

'Me, too, something chronic,' Sid joined in, rubbing one side of his jaw. They both agreed to say that they had toothache and needed to see a dentist. So armed with the word, '*Zahnartz*', they trooped off to see the *Unteroffizier.* He seemed to have had a change of heart and decided to let us all go. He could justify this to his superiors, the deployment of one guard to three prisoners on this occasion. I thought it was marvellous that my two pals were willing to put themselves through this and the likelihood of a German dentist extracting a tooth or two. That was the way people treated toothache then: they pulled the offending tooth out. So the next morning, instead of going to work, we were marched off to Freystadt.

It was a half hour walk or so to the village and we had to make our way to the main road along rough tracks from the farm. We were escorted by this particular guard who was following behind, carrying his rifle down by his side ready to fire if we decided to make a dash for it. I don't know if he was particularly nervous or had been told by somebody that we were a trio of dangerous desperados but we certainly weren't going to give him any trouble. Me with my raging toothache, Laurie and Sid more worried about what was going to happen than making a bid for freedom.

Suddenly, as we were going along the main road, we heard this strange sound in the distance. There was a bend ahead and we couldn't see what was coming. Clump, clump, clump, clump, getting louder. Very odd. The guard knew immediately what it was and shouted, '*Hinunter*!' – get down. We dropped down into the gully by the side of the road and lay there not daring to move. Memories of the road outside Abbeville came back to me as I lay face down in the dirt. I stopped breathing for a moment and listened, trying to make out what was going on.

When we dared to raise our heads up enough to see over the top, I saw a column of 40–50 men and women coming round the bend. They were dressed in dark, filthy clothes that mostly hung off their skinny bodies. The clomping sound was the noise from the wooden clogs they were wearing on their feet. It was a shocking sight. Their faces were white, their eyes sunk right in and they had no hair at all.

There was a guard at the front, behaving as though he was leading a triumphal parade. There were guards either side, some with rifles, others with revolvers in shoulder holsters, holding a whip in one hand which they dragged along the ground and then suddenly cracked. One guard held the lead of an Alsatian dog in his other hand. A guard at the rear held a sub-machine gun, no doubt keeping an eye open for anybody who dropped out or was foolish enough to try and run away.

I couldn't bear seeing this and my temper got the better of me. That red mist of anger, frustration, injustice and helplessness rose before my eyes. It was a bit silly, I suppose, you will probably say I was mad but I jumped out of that gully, scrambled up on to the road and rushed towards one of the guards. '*Schlecht*' – bad, I shouted. 'German culture, bad,' and I spat at the guard's boots. '*Schlecht,*' I moved my head down to spit again.

The guard hardly broke step and the next second, I felt the butt of his rifle hit me hard between my shoulder blades. I collapsed and the pain was so intense like an electric shock that I couldn't breathe. Completely winded. I stayed there on the ground fighting to get my breath back, paralysed, as much from fear as shock. Was a bullet in the head from one of the other guards going to follow?

Poor Laurie and Sid couldn't do anything but watch. If they had got up on to the road and come to help me then they would have got the same treatment or worse; we all could have been shot. By the time I came to and started to get up, these poor devils were away down the road. I could see star shapes and big white patches, the size of dinner plates, stitched on the back of their jackets, which denoted the category of prisoner they were.

Why didn't they try to escape? Even if they got shot, surely that was better than what lay ahead. Going to some God forsaken spot, digging their own graves and then lining up to be shot. Maybe they still hoped that they would get through somehow. I was very, very lucky not be killed. They were almost out of sight when I returned to my pals and the guard.

I didn't care about my toothache any more. My pain now was nothing compared to that of those marching prisoners. We carried on our journey and said not a word about what we had seen there or on the way back. Those poor people in their ill-fitting wooden clogs, walking along that rough road out to their place of death. It made me feel how fortunate I was to be alive and still able to feel the sun on my face and hear the birds singing.

We eventually reached the village and arrived at the dentist's house. My tooth was still hurting but my neck and back were hurting even more. The guard took us into the waiting room where some patients were sitting, and he stood us up against a wall to wait. A women popped her head round a door and called out '*Der Nächste, bitte,'* – next, please, and the guard pushed us all in to the room ahead of those waiting. Nobody protested. A funny little man, who was as wide as he was tall, was standing by the dentist's chair. The woman sat me down, stood in front of me and held both my ears. Strange thing to do, I thought. What was going on? The dentist came round the back and leaned over me.

I hardly had time to open my mouth before the dentist had his pliers inside and had yanked out the rotten tooth. No warning, no anaesthetic, nothing. I screamed. Goodness, the shock of it! I just flipped right out of the chair. When I had recovered enough to stand upright, the woman jammed a piece of lint into my mouth and I held it in place, as blood slowly seeped through onto my hand. I returned to stand by my two very nervous friends for a moment before the guard took me outside.

Poor Laurie and Sid were waiting there, saying to themselves, 'How can I get out of here?' and 'There's nothing wrong with my teeth.' Truth be told, there was something wrong with everybody's teeth. We all had problems as the years passed, with abscesses, gum disease and rotten teeth. No wonder with our poor diet. My teeth (the ones I had left) gradually fell out one by one in the months that followed my return home after the war. I treated myself to a nice pair of dentures. So the dentist did find some rotten teeth to take out. There were no screams coming from Laurie and Sid when it was their turn. They were lucky enough to be given an anaesthetic. My mouth was sore for a while after but I was glad to be rid of that tooth; I could eat properly once again.

Bacon and eggs. Fish and chips. Cheese on toast. What we wouldn't have done to eat just one decent meal like that during our days as POWs. Not eating properly affected us all in different ways and I think it contributed to my erratic behaviour sometimes. My brain and my body were being starved to death. The Germans knew what they were doing when they restricted our food and made us work twelve hours day. Another form of torture. Take away a man's freedom, his dignity and then take away his plate of food.

You do stupid things when you are deprived of the ordinary basic needs of life: sleep, warmth and food. It wasn't just my temper which got me in to trouble. I was mad with hunger, as well as with the unfairness of it all, when I threw down the soup in the farmyard; when I spat at the guard, because of the injustice and cruelty towards those Jews. How else could I make a protest? But it was stupid as I only really punished myself in the end. And it was dangerous. I had not got this far to throw it all away, surely, in a moment of madness?

We knew things would never change and nobody else was going to help us (except the Red Cross), so it was up to us to look after ourselves, keep body and soul together as best as we could. Think of ourselves first, our pals next, family and loved ones after that. We were always talking about home and who we had left behind. Some of the chaps had wives and girlfriends but out of my four pals, I was the only one serious about a girl. This made me even more determined to survive.

Apart from coughs, colds and bouts of diarrhoea, we were lucky not to get seriously ill, even though we never had any medical care or checkups. I do remember, however, on one occasion, that we went out of the camp for some jabs, inoculation against something or other. A group of us were marched to one of the forts a distance away which looked like a pill box with a tower attached where mainly Polish prisoners were kept. We had a long walk down a slope leading underground and then along dark and damp corridors inside this sort of bunker. We lined up in a room and the doctor told us that we were going to receive an injection against TB to be given directly into the chest.

I remember when I awoke next morning I felt as though I had an elephant sitting on my chest. None of us felt like getting up, let alone going out to work. Jimmy was up early as usual and urged us to get moving. We knew the guards could get nasty if you didn't follow orders.

One of the fellows stayed in bed one morning and a guard came in screaming '*Raus, raus*,' – out, out, but he didn't move. Then another guard came in and the two of them pulled him out of the bunk and made him get dressed and marched him outside. The chap was so furious he grabbed a spade, and holding it above his head, went over to one of the guards. Fortunately he saw sense and dropped it. He was lucky not to be put on a charge but was punished by the loss of his bread ration for a week.

It's my opinion that Laurie, Sid, Heb and I owed a lot to Jimmy for the way he kept us going, and saw to it that we didn't starve, both during our years in the camp and on The Long March. There we were surrounded by fields of vegetables, herds of cows and farmyards full of chickens, providing food for Germany's dinner table. How unfair was that? OK, we managed to get a few spuds and mangel-wurzels but that was just cattle fodder.

It was Jimmy who went out on his own at night from time to time and came back with half a bucket of milk for us. I think he must have waited for a particularly moonlit night in order to see what he was doing and not get caught. He knew his way around the farm and where the cows were kept, and somehow he managed to sneak in a shed and coax some milk from them as they stood there. Perhaps the cows weren't even aware of what was going on. We shared that milk among the five of us, enjoying the taste of the warm, frothy milk, a very different taste from the dried KLIM we got in the Red Cross parcels. Wonderful. I would like to say that we saved some for the other chaps but I'm sorry, when you're as hungry as we were, you look after yourself, and there wasn't that much to go around anyway.

Then there were the eggs, another of Jimmy's ideas. We had quite a few over the years, I imagine, enough to share around the whole camp and even a few left for bartering with the locals we had contract with. I suppose it was the nearest thing we had to a cottage industry, our own *Heimindustrie*. Like everything else, this had to be done surreptitiously and carefully. I wouldn't call it stealing exactly as, in a way, we earned those eggs because we put in the work planning it and training the chickens to lay them for us. Because of that, we knew exactly where they were, which made it a lot easier for collecting.

There were chickens running around everywhere, laying perfect organic, free-range eggs. It was a very big farm and there were stables, outhouses and three or four large barns, so the chickens had quite a choice of nesting sites. We weren't free to wander around the farm, looking for likely nesting spots and then just put a few in our pockets and caps to take back home. When we weren't working, we were behind wire fences. However, Jimmy proposed that we trained the chickens to lay eggs in places which would be easy and safe for us to collect. This might be somewhere near where we were working or we passed on our way back from work, or somewhere we could get to easily on a night time excursion through the wire.

One day Jimmy found a smooth, egg-shaped pebble which he thought would make a good fake egg. As a game-keeper, he must have done things like this with the grouse and pheasants in his care on the Highland estate. The plan was to place the pebble in a suitable location to encourage the hens to nest and lay their eggs there. A well-known trick, Jimmy said, as he told us how it worked. Once the hens got used to that place, they would keep returning to lay their eggs there. It worked and they started laying for us.

Somebody would go out every week or so to this secret nesting place and collect the eggs. After a while, we would try another spot and start again, somewhere else handy for us. Keep moving around, don't stick to one place. Don't get complacent and get caught. I don't know if the farmer noticed any reduction in his egg production but we certainly felt the benefit of a bit more protein.

Another opportunity arose, or so we thought, to supplement our meagre rations. It was September and twenty of us had been lent out to another farm some distance away to do some work. We were taken there with two or three guards on horse-drawn carts. As we went along, we were looking at the scenery and talking about where we were going and what we might get for lunch. Food was always a popular subject. The guards weren't taking any notice of us; they didn't understand what we were saying as they never really learned any English. They were more interested in finishing the bread and boiled eggs they had brought with them.

We had travelled quite a long way and were slowing down as we neared our destination. One of our chaps said, 'There's an orchard over there. Looks like loads of smashing plums.' We all turned to look and watched the rows of fruit trees pass by. If only we could get to those trees. Late in the afternoon, after work, we returned to our temporary billet, which was on the second floor of a farm building. The guards couldn't lock us in so three of us decided to go out later when it was dark and try and find these splendid-looking plums. When things were quiet and we thought everybody was asleep, we sneaked downstairs and out, trying not to make the floorboards creak as we went.

I remember that it was a lovely, clear, moonlit night and we could hear the sound of dogs barking in the distance. We went back along the road we had taken, across a couple of fields towards a wooded area which then came out into the orchards. There were row upon row of trees laden with these green plums. 'Victoria plums,' I said, trying to use my knowledge of the fruit trade from Stratford Market. So we started shaking the trees to get the plums down but it didn't seem to be having any effect. They wouldn't budge. 'Not ripe enough probably,' said somebody. By reaching up on tip toes to pull a branch down we managed to get few.

'Oh, God, they're sour,' said one fellow.

'Can't eat these,' said another.

'You know what these are, don't you?' I said. 'Greengages. You can't eat them.' They were as hard as iron and horrible. However hungry you are, there are still some things you cannot eat without making yourself ill. So we left empty handed and made our way back.

We had just crossed a field and were coming up to the main road when we heard men's voices. We dropped right down in the gully at the side and lay down and waited as two men walked past, talking and laughing loudly. When we looked up we saw it was a policeman and a civilian, probably going home after a beer or two in the local bar. They weren't on the lookout for any stray prisoners of war, luckily for us, and when it was safe we made our way to our billet. We didn't get any fruit to eat but we saved ourselves from bellyache from eating the greengages. It was always worth a try when there was the possibility of something to eat and the risk wasn't too great.

Extra rations did come our way, eventually, in an entirely different way. Goodness, what a feast we had! But we nearly get caught.

* * *

It must have been in late 1943, after Italy changed sides and declared war on Germany, that we met a bunch of Italian prisoners down in Freystadt. I was with Laurie, Sid and Jack, unloading coal for the villagers from the railway trucks in the sidings when some Italians walked up the track where we were working. I could hear these lilting voices and unfamiliar language and looked out from the side of the truck to see these men approaching. There didn't seem to be any guards around so we stopped work for a moment. The only person supposed to be guarding us was an elderly civilian who wore a yellow arm band to show he was in charge of us. He lived locally and had gone home to keep warm and have a drink and something to eat. It was a cold day but some of the prisoners had their overcoats hanging over their arms.

They were all smiling and laughing and they waved to us and beckoned us over. We must have looked a real sight with our faces and hands black from coal dust. I wiped my hands as best I could on my trousers, as a gesture of goodwill, and put one out to them. Several came forward to shake hands. '*Ciao, ciao*.'

One of them pointed down the track. '*Ecco, i formaggioni*.'

What? What was he saying? We looked where he was pointing, wondering if there was some trouble further along there.

'*Formaggio*,' said another as he lifted up the edge of his coat to show us what he was carrying under his arm – a large round cheese with a thick brown rind. '*Große Käse*. Che-e-e-s-e.' They wanted to know if we knew that one of the trucks further along had a load of cheeses in it. We four looked at each other and shook our heads. Cheese. That would be good, we thought. It would go down well with the lads back at camp. We managed with a bit of German and a bit of English and a lot of hand waving and body gestures, to communicate with each other.

The Italians told us that they had broken the lock on one of the trucks and climbed inside. They had found some of barrels containing a number of big round cheeses and they had taken some for themselves. They had put the lock back on to make it look as though it was still secure. '*Quattro*,' they said, and one put up four fingers. '*Vier. Numero* four,' – to show how many trucks down the row it was. We thanked them and they thanked us and we shook hands, saying, '*Ciao, ciao*,' back to them and they carried on their way.

'OK, so who fancies going?' said Laurie, rubbing his hands, already planning what he would do with his share of the booty.

'What about you and Sid? Why don't you go?' I said.

'Yes, and I'll stay with Charlie to keep a look out,' said Jack.

The two went off down the track, found the truck and pulled the lock off to open it. They disappeared inside and we kept our eyes skinned for anybody coming. A few minutes later they came back up the line, each carrying a huge cheese. We had taken our coats off before starting work and they were hanging over some railings by the side of the track. There was no need to get them covered in filthy coal dust which was impossible to clean off. Our greatcoats were precious to us. Think what they had been through already and thank heavens for them later on during our long, freezing journey home. And they were always useful for concealing things. Laurie and Sid held the cheeses under their coats which they had over their arms.

Jack and I had finished our work so we put our coats back on. The four of us waited by the side of the road for our guard to return and escort us back to camp. When he eventually turned up, he didn't seem to notice anything different and didn't speak except to say, '*Schnell*,' – quick. He looked as though he'd had a good lunch and a couple of glasses of schnapps.

We were treated like returning heroes back at camp and everybody was excited at the sight of all that cheese. That night we had our own *Käsefest* – cheese festival, and got through an awful lot of it. Don't believe old wives' tales about having nightmares if you eat cheese before bed. I have to say that we fell asleep as soon as our heads hit the board and slept soundly.

However, the next day, before we went out to work, one of the better guards, a decent chap, came to us and warned us that somebody had reported the missing cheeses to the *Bahnpolizei* – Railway Police, and that if we had any cheeses we should get rid of them immediately. I think we had got through about half of each cheese and had put the remainder somewhere out of sight. We realised that this wasn't good enough as a quick search would soon uncover them.

We decided that the best thing to do was to hide them under the floorboards. Nobody would think of looking there. Somebody took up a few floorboards in one of the spare rooms and Jimmy tied some string around each cheese and we lowered them down. Somebody made sure that the end was secured on a nail or something so we could get at them again. We made good the boards and put a table over the area. Lucky we did that, because we didn't have long to wait before the *Bahnpolizei* turned up.

At roll call the next day, we were lined up outside and told to wait. These three policemen appeared in their shiny squeaky boots and pressed trousers and stood in front of us. We waited to hear what was going on. The officer who spoke the best English asked us if we knew anything about a load of cheeses which had been taken from a railway truck. They didn't say how many, and I realised that the police were looking for a number of stolen cheeses. If they discovered ours, we would carry the can for the others which the Italians had taken. That made it a lot more serious.

Nobody said anything. We all looked down at our boots and hoped nothing would give us away. After a few moments of us standing in silence, they went off inside our billet to have a look round. I kept thinking, 'God, I hope they don't smell the cheese.' They didn't stay long, came out, dismissed us and then left. What a relief!

I got back in the evening, having thought about cheese all day long while I was working in the fields. I wasn't the only one looking forward to a bit more with my meal. We needed to eat it up quickly and get rid of all traces now. Somebody went off to get the cheese up from under the floor but when they lifted the boards there was no sign of the cheeses. Disaster! What had happened to them? Rats. When we found the string and pulled it up there was nothing left except bits of brown rind with teeth marks. The rats had eaten a hell of lot in just one night. But that's rats for you. We should have thought of that. Nothing was safe from them.

Rats. Horrible creatures. Always scavenging, looking for food. Night time, that's when they loved coming out. We could hear them all over the building running around. That's why I preferred sleeping on a top bunk. As with a lot of things over the years, we got used to them. It became the norm, whether fleas, lice, mice or rats. Life in this camp, the work we did all year round and the food we ate or didn't eat, made up our world; this was our war and was all that we knew.

That was soon to change. If I had known what lay ahead next, I would have said, 'Let me stay here, safe behind this barbed wire fence.'

12

The Worst Winter

Beautiful but deadly, that's what winter was like. A white landscape with the ghostly shapes of pine trees and rooftops layered with snow like a wedding cake, picture postcard. But stay out in the Arctic winds unprotected and you would die.

Winters were long and hard, lasting from October to March. Dark mornings merged into dark evenings with nothing in between. It felt as though spring and warm weather would never arrive at Langenau and we would be stuck there for ever, forgotten and freezing to death. We spent half our time clearing snow and ice away in order to get out to work and the other half freezing our balls off doing whatever work we were ordered to do outside. The cold and damp got permanently into our bones. No amount of hot soup, burning firewood or layers of clothes would warm us up. I was hardly ever out of my uniform and overcoat during the winter months. I worked and slept in all the clothes I possessed when it was really, really cold.

The army greatcoat was both a curse and a blessing. It was made of dense thick wool and as I got thinner so the coat got bigger and heavier. It flapped about my legs when I was working and it felt like wading in treacle when I made my way along the muddy rows of beets. The coat dragged me down as I bent over further and further with my nose nearly touching the beet tops and my boots stuck in the ground. The bastard Germans had a trick of moving the marker point in the fields from where they had paced out the number of rows we had to do. So when I looked up to see if I had nearly finished there was always another row.

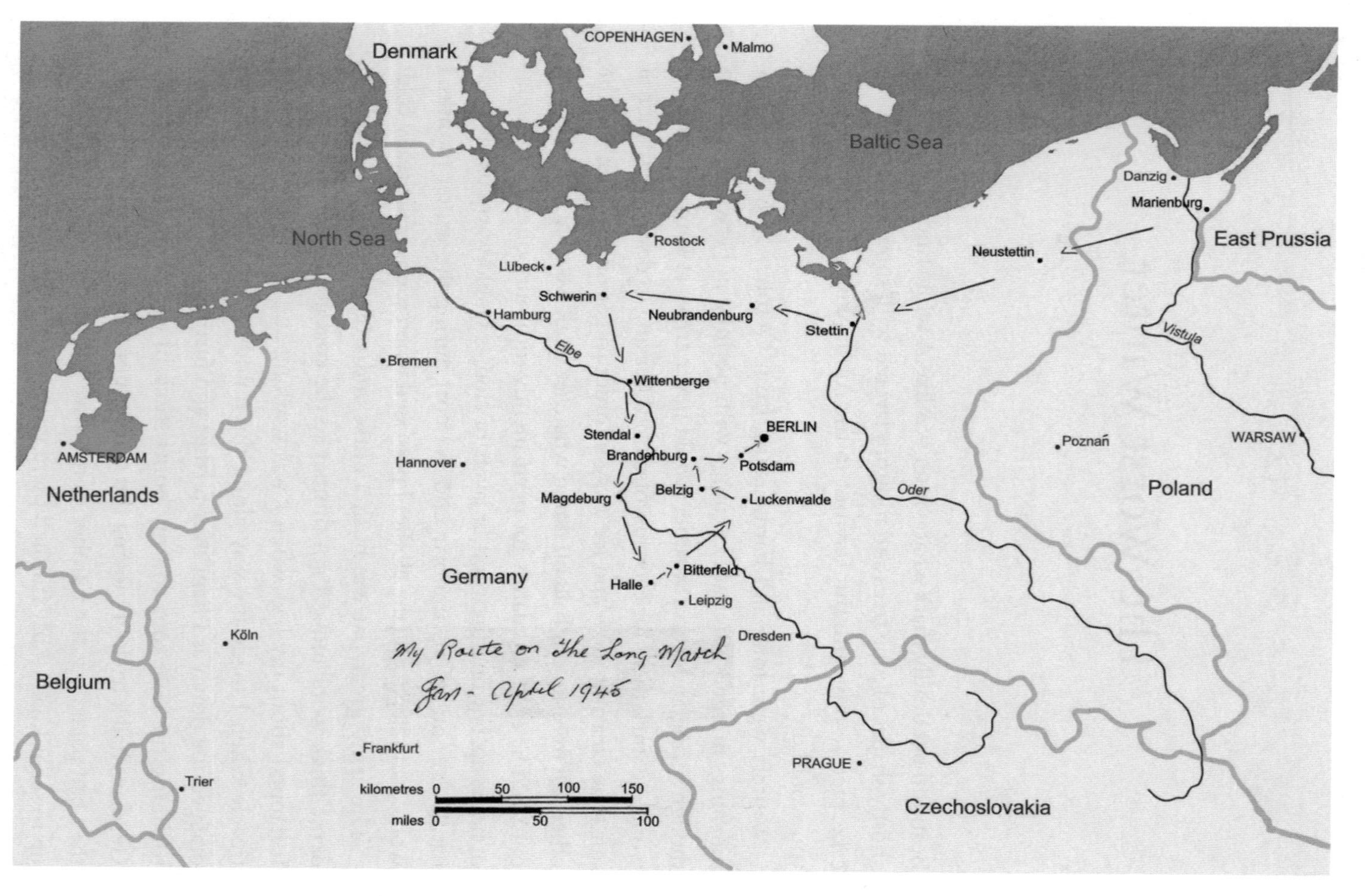

Map of Charles's route on The Long March Jan-April 1945, drawn by Peter Collyer.

On the other hand, we wouldn't have survived without our coats. They were our blanket at night, our defence against the bitter cold by day and an eternal comfort; so they really saved our lives. By God, didn't they keep the wind out! There was room to wear layers of clothes underneath and still be able to move in it. The wide lapels overlapped at the front for extra protection for the chest. With the collar turned up I could keep out the worst of the icy winds. Sleeves were long enough to cover my hands, and pockets big enough to carry my forage cap, eating utensils, identity documents, letters and photos. I still kept Lily close to my heart, her photo in the top breast pocket of my uniform blouse.

19 January 1945. Evening. That's when we heard that we were leaving the camp. When our work parties returned from work, one of the officers called us together and said, 'Pack everything, we're moving'. We had to be ready for six the following morning. Why the hurry? Why did we have to leave at the crack of dawn?

We were going, leaving the only home we had known for nearly five years. You get used to a place, don't you? You get comfortable and get used to your little routines. Never mind that it's a cramped dormitory in a damp house behind barbed wire fences, in the middle of nowhere in a foreign country. Never mind that you eat little and work long hours at gun point; that your hands are blistered and cracked from work and your skin red raw from scratching fleas. You have your mates, your own tiny corner where you can pin up a photo, keep a few bits and bobs, read your letters and be alone with your thoughts.

All that was coming to an end.

The place was abuzz – inside and out. We were excited at the prospect of something happening at last. Prisoners and guards were busy, men everywhere trying to get their things together, sort themselves out. There were chaps looking for stuff they had saved or hidden for a rainy day. Now was that rainy day – or rather snowed-in day. We five set to work straightaway as we talked and sorted what belongings we had.

'Another camp,' said Laurie. 'Wonder what they've got in store for us.'

'Nothing good,' said Heb.

'A change is as a good as a rest,' said Sid.

'It's freezing out there!' I said. Little did we know that the winter of 1945 turned out to be one of the worst of the twentieth century with temperatures falling as low as -25°c. 'Abso–bloody-lutely freezing!' I added.

Jimmy echoed my sentiments with something incomprehensible.

'Hope it's not far,' said Heb. 'I'm exhausted just thinking of going.'

We all thought we were moving to another work place. We had no idea that the Russians were advancing and the war was coming to an end. It would have been so much better for us if we had known what was going on so we could have made plans. Bloody silly time to move. Why couldn't they wait until the weather got better? We had no idea what was in store.

I had never really stopped to think about what would happen at the end of the war. I always wondered how we would know it was over and how we would get back to England. I didn't imagine that it would end like this – our journey back to freedom and civilisation.

As soon as we left the camp and passed through the gates and wire fences, we realised we weren't off to another work place. Everybody was there – officers, guards, the lot – and we knew something big was happening. No idea where we were going but I just knew this looked like big trouble. Memories of that first march from Abbeville to Trier and journey by the cattle truck came back to me. That's where it had all started.

I did the silliest thing when I knew we were leaving. Like everybody else we wanted to take everything we had. Over time fellows had collected or made quite a few knick knacks and souvenirs: matchstick models, animals and figures whittled from wood, stones picked and polished. Some had Red Cross boxes and bags that they had begged, borrowed or stolen. I got into one of the barns where I remembered seeing some storage boxes. That'd be good for carrying my stuff, I thought. I didn't expect we were going far. If I could find a really strong cardboard box, not too heavy, I would put all my belongings in it.

My letters were the most precious things I possessed and I had a real stack of them. Nearly five years' worth. I wasn't going to leave them behind. I had odds and ends left from my last Red Cross parcel (bit of chocolate, some biscuits and a few cigarettes). I had my spoon and bowl, shaving kit, towel, bit of soap, spare pair of socks, trousers and my old boots.

I decided to wear my new boots which my mother had sent me, and keep the old ones as spare. Because of the extreme cold, I was already wearing pretty much all the clothes I owned including my spare underwear and my fireman's jumper over my uniform. I packed my old boots and everything else neatly inside the box and tied it up with some string – the stuff made from twisted brown paper which came with the Red Cross parcels. I was ready to go.

What on earth did I look like? There I was holding this huge box out in front as though I was Father Christmas looking for some kiddies to give them their presents. I soon realised how stupid I was. There I was battling through the snow drifts against the icy winds, my arms aching and my feet skidding on the slippery ice-impacted roads as I tried to keep up with the other men marching out into the white wilderness.

I wasn't alone though in trying to carrying everything. Nobody had said, 'Look, men, take only what you can eat or wear. Dump everything else.' It could have saved a lot of trouble later on. Me and the other chaps soon started throwing things away as we went along, to lighten our load and make it easier to walk and not fall behind the column. We kept the absolute essentials and ditched everything by the roadside. God, how I wish we could have kept it all. We had little enough to show for our five years of slave labour but it was all precious to us.

So that was how I came to lose all my letters and cards from home and most of my photos. I kept two envelopes, from mother and Lily's last letters, and placed a couple of family photos inside along with my Army Service Pay Book. I'm looking at the Pay Book now. It's not actually in that bad a condition considering what it went through; amazing it has survived. The cover is creased and water stained and it still smells of tobacco smoke. On the inside pages I can read about the vital statistics of my younger self, that I weighed 130lbs and was medical classification 'A' on enlistment. I can also pride myself that I fulfilled the Instructions to Soldiers 'You will always carry this book on your person.' I had my dog tag round my neck, the belt my friend made from the tops of old army boots round my waist and everything else stuffed into my many pockets.

Jimmy, of course, was better equipped. He was born to be out of doors and always on the go. Like a good Boy Scout, or gamekeeper, I should say, he knew to 'be prepared'. He always carried an assortment of useful things about his person: stub of pencil, needle, matches, knife, bits of old wire and string. And on The March, true to form, he was always on the lookout for things to make our lives better, opportunities to search the area and any empty houses along the way.

When we left camp Jimmy had a rucksack made from a hessian animal feed bag on his back. I'm not sure if he had found the bag and stitched it together himself or our tailor friend had made it. He kept all his stuff in there including his tartan trews, which he changed into when the weather got better months later and the sun was shining. I enjoyed watching him up in front, head held high, tartan legs striding along, and the ribbons on his Highland cap fluttering behind.

> 39 men.
> Left the farm at Langenau [20 January] 2 men stay in hiding.
> Everybody in good spirits.

It was Saturday (one of our rest days) when the camp was evacuated. No rest for us though. We had started with forty-five men in the camp back in 1940, lost a few, gained a few and were down to forty-one. When the officer took the roll call there were two men missing and a couple of guards were sent to look for them. Our two chaps didn't appear and we never heard any shots fired so maybe they got away. God knows where they went. To the coast to find a boat? Madness. In the end the guards were called back and we set off on foot down the road.

The Germans had loaded two small horse-drawn carts – one full of supplies, including some Red Cross parcels, and their equipment; the other nearly empty. This was later used to fetch bread from villages where a bakery was still in business, and also to carry those too ill or injured to walk. I remember looking at the horses thinking they looked in better condition than us. There were bags of feed on the cart for them but it wasn't enough for a long journey in the middle of winter.

Of course, the guards were more worried about keeping the horses fed than us prisoners. We felt sorry for the creatures. They were doing a good job so we kept an eye open for hay when we stopped off somewhere. If we kipped in a barn or stable we grabbed a handful of straw and fed them when we could. I remember Laurie saying, after we'd been a month on the road when everybody, including the horses, looked on their last legs: 'If one of the nags goes down, at least we're in with the chance of a decent meal.' Those horses turned out to be lot tougher than us.

[21 January] March 42km. Nearly all of us throw away a lot of kit. Much too heavy to carry

It was on the second day that the dreadful weather conditions got the better of us and I and most of the other men realised the folly of struggling to carry bundles, boxes, bags, whatever, of belongings. Nearly everybody started throwing things away as they went along. You could look back and see a trail of discarded items. During an early stop, I said, 'I can't be doing with this!' and tipped out the box leaving everything in the snow except my bit of food, cigarettes, piece of soap, socks, and my spoon and bowl. What I couldn't fit into my already full coat pockets got left behind.

Survival. That was what we focussed on. You concentrated on the walking, watching your feet and the boots of the men in front and getting into the rhythm. Nobody wanted to fall behind. God help you if you got detached. And when other groups of men gradually joined us along the way, it was even more important to stick together and not get separated. Even though we hadn't a clue where we were going, we thought, 'Better the devil you know. Stick with your mates.'

We were fortunate, my pals and I, to be at the back of the line so the first men in front were clearing a path which made it easier for us. We still had to battle through deep snow sometimes up to our chests, sometimes digging it away by hand, other times stopping to get shovels off the back of cart while the guards looked on. It was exhausting. Every icy breath drawn in hurt your lungs and made your teeth and head ache. Every movement was painful. Every step dangerous. It was so slippery that you had to watch every step so you didn't fall. I thought about our horses at home, how I used to take them to the blacksmith's in winter to have studs put in their shoes for the bad weather. We could have done with some of those on our boots to give us a bit of grip. It was never this like in Essex even during the worst winters. Such a struggle just to be able to walk a few hundred metres. Would there ever be an end to this torture?

Always the snow and the ice. It was the continuous gnawing cold which made your eyes water except the tears froze and glued your lids together. Even with a scarf wrapped round, your cap on, and coat collar up, your head ached as though somebody was banging an ice cold hammer through your brain. Even with two pairs of socks on, your feet were so cold you had to look down and check that they were still there at the end of your legs. Even if you had gloves or your homemade mittens on and stuffed your hands deep into your pockets you could still feel them burning with cold as though they were being held over a hot flame. Utterly, utterly miserable.

There was a plan of sorts – to go in a westerly direction from camp to camp – but it didn't always work out like that. We didn't know the route and I don't think the guards did either half the time. Sometimes we walked for days in huge circles coming back to where we started. Cries went up: 'Christ in heaven, we've been here before!' or 'Where in f------ hell are we going?' but it made no difference. We just carried on. We followed orders. With guards carrying machine-guns you just did. No questions asked. In spite of having walked all day, it was so cold that gangs of men got into circles at night to keep warm and continued walking round and round; others were so frightened to lie down and go to sleep that they used to prop each other up as they snatched a few minutes sleep here and there.

Not long after we started on The March, we began picking up other POWs – twenty, thirty or forty men at a time, until we had a steady column of about 100–150 men. It was a shifting and changing group. Some stayed a few days to rest or work and moved off again and some others would join us. Some of our original guards stayed for quite a while but as time went on, older men replaced the younger ones who left, called back to fight the Allied advance from the west and the Russian Army from the east.

One of the first groups to join us was a bunch of American airmen who were pulling homemade sledges. They seemed very well-prepared with woolly hats and scarves wrapped round their heads and some had fur mittens, even goggles. We were very envious of them with their belongings packed neatly on the sledges even though it was probably quite difficult pulling them along on the ice and through the thick snow.

They looked pretty fit and well fed to me and we learned that they had only been prisoners for three months. When we told them how long we had been POWs they were shocked. 'Jeez, no wonder you guys look like death warmed up!' They could see in our haggard faces that we had suffered a lot. Of course, most Yanks love the Brits and everything British and as they had been stationed over in England they waxed lyrical about our countryside and village pubs but mainly our food. 'Oh, we love your fish and chips' and 'How about those steak and kidney pies?' How much they missed them. If they missed them, what about us? I did think it was insensitive of them going on about our wonderful food when we were starving but at least they shared a cigarette or two with us and a bit of chocolate. One good thing about smoking was that it curbed your appetite. Our stomachs had shrunk over the years so we were used to eating very little but it was still hard, very hard to cope in these conditions.

Our bits and pieces from the Red Cross parcels were soon eaten up and we relied on the handouts of stale bread distributed by the guards. Keeping warm by moving was more important than eating. You didn't want to sit down or your trousers would freeze to the ground. You didn't want to take your hands out of your pockets even if you had strips of old blanket wound round them because the tips of your fingers would get frostbite. At times groups managed to clear a small area and light a fire or two and make a brew with melted snow and a few tea leaves from someone's pocket. We would pass the bowl around the lucky men in the group. It reminded me of happier times felling trees in the Rosenberg forest.

Hebby managed to make notes during the journey in a diary which he had taken from the blacksmith's where he had worked. He kept track of places and distances we covered. I don't know how he worked out how far we walked each day because we didn't always see sign posts or know which places we'd been through but he was the sort of person who kept his eyes peeled, listened to other people and picked up information that way. What he wrote down helped me when I jotted down my own notes using the blank pages of my New Testament. I brought this home with me but it was not the original one with which every soldier was issued on enlistment. I was given this book about a week into the March by a padre I met in a church. It is stamped inside *Stalag 2B Geprüft* – meaning 'examined', so it came from another camp.

> I received this [New Testament] on 28th Jan 1945
> During a halt on The March
> About 1,000 of us in a church.
> One of our boys is now playing the organ

As we walked on and on through villages and towns we began to see the effects of the war and the damage caused by the Allied bombing raids. It was dusk, after another long day walking, when we came to a large town or the outskirts of a city. It looked much the same as all the other places in the evening gloom with smashed vehicles – carts and cars, boarded up buildings, empty houses and deserted streets. There was a church standing in a square littered with stones and rubble. Some of the guards went ahead and must have checked it out because we started moving slowly in that direction. It was large with fancy stonework and buttresses and steps up to the main doors.

As usual we were at the back of the column following the others in straggly groups as they made their way towards the entrance. It took us a while to get there so we were the last to go in. Somewhere dry for the night. Fantastic! A couple of guards were having a quick smoke and then moved on inside. When we got in through the big heavy front door it was dark inside. We were in a wide, narrow, dark vestibule with steps and passageways off to the side. In the gloom I could make out the shapes of fellows hunched up asleep in a corner and moved past them towards the inside door. Sid and Heb were ahead, already poised to open it and go inside the church.

It was Jimmy, of course, who spotted it, always on the lookout for opportunities to make his and our lives better. He obviously had an idea.

'Look, Chas,' he said pointing to this full length plush red velvet curtain which was pushed back to the side of the door into the church. 'What d'yer think?' I nodded, wondering what he had in mind. It was thick and heavy and wouldn't be easy to handle. What on earth were we going to do with it?

'We can get it down.' He looked at Laurie and me. We nodded. 'It'll be heavy to carry.' It seemed mad to me but I knew Jimmy well enough not argue.

'OK, then,' I said. 'I'll do it.'

Sid and Heb came back to see what was going on and Jimmy told them to go and have a scout round. 'What we need is a long bit o' wood. A pole or something.' He turned to me. 'Quick, on my shoulders before anyone sees.'

I was the smallest and the lightest, although to be honest, we were all as thin as the wooden window pole which Sid and Heb came back with. Jimmy cupped his hand for me to get up and then pushed me up onto his shoulders and manoeuvred me towards the top of the door. I clenched my thighs firmly round his neck.

'All right, Jimmy?' I said, wobbling a bit. 'Steady there, man.'

I managed to take the curtain off the hooks attached to the heavy rings on the metal rail and give it an almighty tug. 'Timber!' shouted

Jimmy as the massive curtain flew past his head nearly landing on Laurie below. Laurie caught it and started trying to sort it out. I jumped down and between the three of us we managed to fold it over and over until it formed a tight bundle. Jimmy had some twine in his pocket – proper stuff, not the soggy brown paper nonsense from the Red Cross parcels, which he tied round the curtain to secure it.

'That'll do. Gi'us here.' Jimmy grabbed the pole from Sid and pushed it through the centre of the bundle. 'There you go.' He and Laurie lifted it up.

'Look, Dick Whittington!' said Sid.

We all looked at each other again still puzzled.

'That'll keep us cosy at night,' said Jimmy.

Ah, yes, of course.

Nobody had noticed all this kerfuffle of ours in the vestibule – or cared, thank goodness. We got away with it.

It was warm inside the church, probably because of the huge number of men packed in. I reckoned on a thousand there leaning, lying, squatting and sitting in every space and corner. They were in the aisles, the pews, up the pulpit, on the tombstones, against the altar. But there was room, there's always room for one more. Wherever we went over the next months, however crowded it was – whether stables or pig sty, bombed-out railway station or church, you could always squeeze in a few more.

As Sid, Heb and I made our way carefully over the sleeping men on the stone floor, Laurie and Jimmy carried the pole between them like Indian bearers for a memsahib. Suddenly the organ burst into life and this terrific sound of music filled the church. A verse of *Onward Christian Soldiers* followed by the chorus of *Roll out the Barrel*. It was Jack, the one who played the piano accordion in our camp. So his hours of practice weren't wasted. He had found a way into the organ loft and couldn't resist having a go. People started cheering and clapping at the music.

After a final flourish of *I Do Like to be Beside the Seaside* and more applause (and a few cries of 'Shut the f---- up!') Jack came back down and managed to work his way through the mass of bodies to join us where we had settled down. He didn't want to be separated from us. No good going off with another group in the morning. Never knew where you might end up. Even though we didn't have a clue how, when or where it would end, it was better sticking with the mates you knew from all the years together than risk something worse with a bunch of strangers.

The doors of the church were locked. We five settled down in a side chapel near our own men. All looking forward to a good night's sleep. Safe and dry. Sid and I propped ourselves up against a sculptured monument. I was squeezed up against another fellow who turned to me and put out his hand. 'Harry,' he said.

I returned the handshake, 'Charlie. Nice to meet you.'

'And you. Would you like a Bible?'

'OK,' I said. It would have been mean to say no to a padre.

He reached in his backpack and took out a small testament and gave it to me. 'I've got a spare one.' He smiled. 'It's always good to have God on your side,' he said.

'Yes,' I said, 'I need all the help I can get.'

Nothing, not even hundreds of coughing, grunting and snoring men, or the foot of a stone angel pressing into my back, could stop me from falling asleep straightaway. Jimmy and Laurie were curled up together and had the luxury of the velvet bundle as a pillow that night but from then on, two of us took it in turns to carry it and we used it as a ground cover and a blanket wherever we went.

Imagine the comfort and warmth of plush velvet round you as you slept in the open air, under a hedge or in a cattle byre. We managed to carry it for the next six weeks until we found it too exhausting and had to leave it behind. A real shame but I'm sure somebody else benefited from it when they too looked for shelter and found our velvet curtain neatly folded up on the ground.

13

Body and Soul

When I look at the notes I jotted down all those years ago on The March and trace the route now on a map, it looks absolutely crazy. How did I do it? How did I keep going all that way?

We made our way along the Baltic coast from our camp near Marienburg, on to Neustettin, crossing the river Oder at Stettin where the bridge was blown up soon after. On to Nuebrandenburg, in the direction of Lübeck where we had heard there were a million Red Cross parcels. We got as far as Schwerin and turned south towards Wittenberge. We walked across the frozen river Elbe, at some point, on to Stendal, further south to Magdeburg and Halle (just north of Leipzig). We zig -zagged across to Luckenwalde, Belzig, north west to Brandenburg, eastwards to Potsdam and finally in the direction of Berlin. Goodness me, what a journey! I must have covered about 1600km.

On we went, sometimes just a step ahead of the bombing raids, other times soon after. We passed civilians and soldiers going both ways – like us, looking for somewhere safe to go. What else could we do but keep going? We were marching at gun point so we didn't argue, following wherever we were led. The officers tried to plan the day's march and rest stops. An officer would send a party of guards ahead to look for somewhere suitable for the night. It might be a barn or stables or in more populated areas, they found railway stations, churches, factories and the remains of bombed buildings. Later we found ourselves commandeered to clear bombed areas and railway lines, doing yet more slave labour for our German masters.

Thank God for a decent pair of boots! My army issue boots had seen me through a hell of lot over the past five years. Now my lovely new soft leather boots, the best quality my mother could afford, would do the same. Unlike the army issue ones, which had to be broken in, mine gave me no trouble. They were a perfect fit and I managed to keep them in good order on The March. Without them I would have been in deep trouble. Look after your boots and they will look after your feet. If you can stay upright and just keep going then you had a good chance of getting through it all.

And that's what I did: kept going.

A lot of men were not so lucky. There were fellows with dreadfully worn-out shoes which let in the wet and rotted their feet; some didn't have anything to wear and had bits of material wrapped round their feet like bandages. I heard of somebody who had his wooden work clogs on when his camp was suddenly evacuated and his feet were permanently damaged by wearing them. So good boots were essential to your health and survival.

The most important thing to remember was not to take off your boots, not just because of the fear of frostbite, and your toes going black, but because they could get stolen or you might never get them back on your feet. Sad to say, it was every man for himself out there. If you left your boots somewhere at night they would be gone by morning. If you were lucky and they were still there, either your feet would have swollen so much or the leather frozen solid over night, or both, that you wouldn't be able to get them back on. If you couldn't walk, and your mates couldn't carry you, and the cart was full of the injured, sick and dying, then you were left behind.

Keeping warm was also a matter of life and death. I didn't take my clothes off for at least six weeks. I walked all day and slept all night in them. I was in a shocking state most of the time. Never mind the stink; everybody was in the same boat. Not washing or shaving, hair and beard matted with filth, skin crawling with fleas and lice. My skin hurt, red raw from me scratching through my clothes or at any bits of exposed flesh. Like so many things in my life – during those lost years of imprisonment,

I got used to it. It became normal. There were more important things to worry about anyway. We didn't dare take our clothes off or we would have died of cold so we tried to keep every part of ourselves covered as much as possible. Nobody wanted to get frostbite or catch pneumonia. When the weather got better and everything started to melt, there was plenty of water around to have a quick wash in a puddle or stream, however basic it was.

Later we stopped at stalags en route and work sites and, when the weather was better, if there was a tap or stand pipe it was a treat to wash your face and hands. We didn't dare take off our clothes and certainly not our underwear when we got a delousing.

[16 March]

Sid, Laurie & myself just deloused.

An important enough event, I made a note of it on the back of the group camp postcard I had kept with me. I think all we got was a puff of DDT powder on our heads, down our underpants and inside our vests. I don't remember where that happened or who did it. Somebody obviously took pity on us or just didn't want any more lousy prisoners around. But of course it made no difference as the blighters all came back pretty well straightaway. Same clothes (unwashed), same sleeping arrangements (cheek by jowl) and same fleas (offspring ready for action).

Now lying in barns waiting to move again

The best place to settle down for the night was somewhere with straw. If you were lucky and found a barn or hay loft, you could climb up and bury yourself in the hay. Lovely stuff. You could move it like sheets and then tuck your feet under. It wasn't warm, it was boiling. Marvellous. Imagine walking all day in thick snow and in the freezing cold and finding that for bedding. Wonderful. Failing that, a cowshed would do with cows preferably because they gave off so much heat. Failing that, huddle up with your pals or anybody; you couldn't afford to be choosy. It was Shakespeare, I believe, who wrote, 'Misery acquaints a man with strange bedfellows' and I certainly experienced that first-hand.

If you couldn't keep warm it was even more important to make sure you kept eating – anything to keep your strength up. Years as a POW conditioned me to starvation rations and my stomach shrank considerably. I learned to eat whatever was put in front of me and make the most of what I was given or I scrounged or stole. Obviously I learned my lesson the hard way when I turned my nose up at that cold soup served on the farm the day, when I chucked it on the ground and was attacked by Jan, the guard. No point in being squeamish or fussy about what you put in your mouth or you would starve to death.

The thought of food was always in our minds. Every minute of the day and night, waking in the early hours with a gnawing pain inside from the hunger. Jimmy, Laurie, Sid, Heb and I were used to eating rubbish food, with the occasional luxury of a Red Cross parcel and extra farm produce we nicked. Searching for food (anything edible) was second nature to us. Even more important than before in these harsh conditions. We had no idea what was round the next corner.

We preferred keeping at the back of the group, trailing behind the long straggly column of men, with the guards spread out ahead. We were able to go off on our own or in pairs to forage – like our night raids through the barbed wire fence. There were farm buildings and empty houses where the owners had fled and we checked for food and water. Then we caught the group up and shared our booty or kept it until we stopped for the night.

Fields were deep in snow and ground frozen solid so it was impossible to find anything edible growing. I do remember, however, eating raw turnips (ghastly because they gave you belly ache), dock leaves, sour as crab apples, and wild chives. It might be only four or five mouthfuls but it kept you going. We searched pig sties. I ate stinking, rotten left-over pig swill from troughs and examined slurry for scraps. I found some tiny, small potatoes in the mud and shit and took handfuls to a stream where I washed them. I filled my pockets up and we had them baked on a piece of tin over a fire that night. We all played our part in finding extra life-saving food.

One day Laurie and I were looking round some old farm buildings when we heard a squealing noise. Laurie went to investigate and came back with a little piglet under his arm which was struggling to escape. There was a metal drum nearby so Laurie got the piglet by its back legs, swung it hard, smashing its head against the side. Bang! Killed instantly. I did feel sorry for the little creature. I know it was necessary but I couldn't have done it, not even to save my life. Laurie was a butcher in civvy street and not squeamish about animals – dead or alive.

We returned to the group and Laurie had the dead piglet under his coat. 'Pork for supper,' he said, opening his coat an inch to show the others. When we stopped for the night, it was Laurie's job to cut up the carcass and we roasted it in the fire. I don't know when we had last eaten any meat. What a glorious smell! Roast pork and crackling. Fat dripping down into the fire making the flames spit. Oh, the taste! We had a fine meal that night and there were even a few scraps left for our friends.

I was only a greengrocer's assistant after all. What would you expect me to do? I couldn't have done without Laurie the time I found the fish heads. We were passing through a village and I was looking around, keeping half an eye open for the guards when I came across a dustbin left on the pavement. The others were up ahead so I stopped for a quick look. I lifted the lid, peered inside and saw a load of fish heads among the rubbish. I wondered how long they had been there. I would have to see what the others had to say. So I picked about a half a dozen out and wrapped them in a bit of newspaper which was inside and carried the packet stuffed inside the front of my coat.

'What you reckon?' I said to Laurie as I pulled out the packet and peeled back the paper. We both took a sniff.

'I think they'll be all right,' he said. 'Give 'em a try.'

'Yes, but I can't take the eyes out.' You wouldn't have thought after all that business, I would be afraid to remove the eyes. I didn't mind watching my brother Alfred removing his glass eye to clean it. What was the difference?

'Don't worry, Charlie, I'll do it.' Laurie was as good as his word.

We stopped that night in part of a disused factory and groups of men lit fires and settled to brew up or cook a meal, depending on what they had found or had brought with them. I took the fish heads out and Laurie laid them on the piece of tin kept for cooking. Laurie borrowed a needle from Jimmy which he kept on a lapel and delicately picked out each eyeball and threw it in the fire. Pop, pop they went. The heads only took a moment to cook so we soon had them to eat. Only a tiny piece each, more like an appetizer, except we had no main course to follow. Still it was tasty.

We would be walking along as usual when one of us would look round and say, 'Where's Jimmy?' He was always slipping off somewhere unnoticed. Nowhere to be seen. Then he would re-appear with something he had found.

One day, Jimmy was checking out houses to see if there was anybody about. Not that people being at home put him off going in. Sometimes we arrived in a village not long after the civilians had fled after another bombing raid or in fear of Russian troops arriving. Some men slept in the abandoned houses but my pals and I never did. Jimmy went into one cottage which was empty and looked around the kitchen and found some jugged geese legs, preserved in an earthenware jar, on a shelf in a cupboard. He hid it under his coat and brought it back. Sounds strange but they were delicious heated up. I would have eaten them cold. I wasn't fussy. Pity we had to ditch the jar, as it might have come in handy, but it was too heavy to carry.

Rations very bad. Everybody hungry and weak.

Our planes are bombing every day and night.

Another time, what did Jimmy bring back? Before we had time to miss him he appeared carrying a milk churn. He had been into a cottage to look around and had found two loaves of bread. He grabbed them and when he got outside put them in a churn to hide them from the guards or anybody else who would try to take them away. We had a lot of bread that night. Bread was always an important part of our diet and if we weren't getting our ration from the Germans because their supply had dried up, it was every man for himself.

If the Germans managed to get fresh bread it was of course as much for them as for us. What they did was to send one of the carts ahead with a couple of armed guards to order loaves from the baker in the next town 8 or 10km away– if there was one still in business. The baker didn't have any choice. The officer would work out how many loaves were needed for the hundred or so of us plus the guards. They had a loaf between two of them while we shared a loaf with eight or more. When we arrived at the village the bread would be waiting and we would collect it and then be on our way. It was such a treat when you lined up later in the day and got your slice of bread from a loaf.

However, on more than one occasion, the price of that bread was half a brick thrown at your head.

As we marched through villages and towns, civilians would come out of their houses and throw stones and bricks at us. Because we were British (or French, Belgian or American, they didn't know) and prisoners of war. Two days before this, our planes had been over and smashed their homes, killed their people so it wasn't surprising how they felt; they were bound to be resentful and want to get their own back. This meant that the German guards escorting us were also getting struck by these missiles, so they had to do something to stop it – for their own sakes if not for ours.

Half a dozen guards would go ahead of the marching column, machine guns at the ready to make sure there was nobody outside ready to throw stones or bricks at us. The last thing they wanted was casualties because that would be a burden on us all. The cart was full most of the time with injured and ill men. It slowed us down. We had to stop to tend to them until we reached the next camp or wherever it was we could leave them to be looked after.

A bit of bread kept body and soul together. Kept us moving. On and on. Kept those legs moving. The things we did for a bite to eat. I stole a piece of bread from somebody. One night we were sleeping in an old barn, all huddled up together and I was the one on the end of the row. We used to take it in turns as that was the coldest spot. I saw this chap next to me tuck a chunk of bread under his coat which he was using as a pillow. When he was facing away from me, I reached out and slipped my fingers under the coat and took it out. That's how bad it was. Stealing from a fellow prisoner. No good trying to share it with my pals as I would have had to move and then draw attention to myself. This chap would soon realise what was going on. I wolfed the bread down but I didn't enjoy eating it.

Each day one of us took charge of the water can, sometimes our only supply during the day if we were able to get it filled. On one of his house visits, Jimmy had found a miner's lamp with a handle and a lid and he adapted it to use for carrying water. I think it was later on our journey, when the weather was better and the roads were dry, probably the middle of March when we were going through another small village. There were eight cottages ranged in pairs with a gap between. Laurie, Sid and Heb were up ahead; Jimmy and I loitering behind. I was looking around when something caught my eye. I pulled at Jimmy's sleeve.

'Hang on, Jimmy,' I said, 'I think there's a pump.' I was in charge of the water can that day. I thought I had seen one round the back of a cottage and would take the opportunity to try and fill it up.

'OK, Chas, you catch us up.' He left me and carried on walking.

I walked across to the cottages which all looked empty and rundown, gardens untended and rubbish all around as though families have left in a hurry. I went down between two cottages to the back into a cobbled yard where I saw this pump. So I grabbed this rusty old handle and I was trying it first to see if it worked, pulling it up and down, up and down. It was squeaking, making an awful racket. 'Come on, come on. Water. Water. Quick,' I said out loud. That's all I needed, somebody to hear me and catch me in the act.

All of a sudden the back door of the cottage opened and a man called out '*Guten Tag,*' – good day.

So I said, '*Guten Tag.*' Oh God, he'd caught me. What was I going to do?

Then he called out '*Wohin gehst du?*' – where are you going?

I didn't know what to say so I replied, '*Ich weiss nicht.*' – I don't know.

Then I saw that he was coming out of the house and down the path towards me. I decided to stop pumping and walked towards him and met him half way.

'*Einen Augenblick,*' – wait a minute, he said, signalling with his hands for me to stay there. He turned and went back indoors and I waited a couple of minutes before he came out again carrying a small packet wrapped up in newspaper. He held it out to me, '*Für Sie*' – for you, and pushed it towards me and said, '*Viel Glück,*' – good luck, '*Sehr viel Glück,*' – lots of luck.

I opened it carefully, not sure what I was going to find and took a quick look. I could see some homemade biscuits and half a dozen hand-rolled cigarettes. I thanked him, '*Vielen Dank,*' adding '*Sehr gütig,*' – very kind.

As I walked away, I looked back over my shoulder and saw this poor old man, still standing there outside this run-down old cottage. I felt bad. He hadn't got much himself. He probably thought I was German because I managed a few words in his language. There was a German unit called the *Arbeitsteam* – working party, in the area. They also wore a khaki uniform when on duty, similar to ours. I reckoned that was what he thought I was. He was giving me something to help his side. I answered his questions truthfully. I didn't know where we were going and I got away with it. But I felt sorry because as he turned to go back inside, I glimpsed an old lady, his wife, I imagined, through the half-open door, lying inside on a little camp bed.

Everybody else had gone, had left the place but she was too ill or too old to leave and so they stayed. Poor man, he thought he was helping a German. But then again, he might not have minded. Perhaps he just saw someone in a similar position to himself and did what he thought was right. I was worried that the Russians were not far behind and fearful of what would happen to them when they arrived. He and his wife had done nothing wrong. They were victims too, just like the rest of us.

I held out the parcel to Jimmy. 'See what I've got.'

'Did you get the water, Chas?'

'Oh, shit! I forgot.'

Still, we all had a good smoke, sharing a couple of the ciggies, bartering the rest for some extra bread from a guard.

* * *

27 February 1945. It was a brilliant moonlit night when we crossed the frozen river Elbe. There was a full moon which shone like a search light, illuminating everything in a mysterious ghostly glow. We couldn't see the other side so it was an act of a faith to cross where we did because it could have been miles wide.

There were people making their way across this frozen highway going in both directions so this was obviously a good sign; our guards must have thought that we could all get across. There wasn't any bridge; it was just one foot in front of the other slow and sure, all the way across the frozen water. If I had fallen through the ice that would have been it. I would have drowned or died of hypothermia. This was a different sort of cold. Imagine this: the freezing cold under your feet, rising up your legs and into your body; and all around, air like needles of ice in your eyes and face, in your nose, your throat and lungs. It literally took your breath away.

It was best not to look down and think about what I was walking on. Some of us held on to each other to keep steady. We just had to keep going as though it was the most normal thing in the world, to be walking on a skating rink. I told myself it was like going along the High Street or down Movers Lane as we passed other people. There was us, with our German guards, leaving the east to get away from the Russian advance, and we were passing German soldiers going west to meet the Red Army.

I did feel sorry for the civilians I saw. There was a family carrying all their worldly possessions piled up in a small hand cart; others with a couple of back packs and a basket. A woman with a baby all swaddled up inside the front of her coat clutched her husband's hand as he tried to keep his balance with a large bundle strapped to his back. We passed an elderly couple hunched over in the cold struggling under the weight of the loads. They had two cows with them and they had put sacks on the ice under the creatures' feet and were trying to keep the animals moving and the sacks in place under their hooves, so they didn't slip. How long it took them to cross, I don't know. What hardship these poor folk suffered! They had lost everything except what they had with them.

It was possibly half a mile to a mile walk across to the other side of the river. We found somewhere to rest for a while and then continued our journey, going south as we made our way towards – where? Nobody knew. Sometimes you just wanted to sit down and never get up again but common sense prevailed and your pals pulled you up onto your feet and off you went. A few more camps on the way, more bombed towns, lines of men marching, more zig-zagging towards some unknown destination.

March 6
Still on March
At present having a few days rest.
Have received Red X
1 parcel 2 men
1 parcel 3 men.

We never knew when or where we would stop for the night and whether we would find anything decent to eat. I know we received some Red Cross parcels along the way; presumably at the stalags. We were certainly owed a few from the many times we never received our fair share at Langenau. Later on when we were ordered to clear up bombed sites, we had some proper meals from field kitchens which had been set up. It was like being back in a work detachment. We were in no fit state to work, but we had to. Exhausted and weak as we were at least it was a change from the marching and relief for our poor old feet. More importantly, there was the chance of some real hot food.

March 16

Today's dinner (few spuds in jackets)

Boiled barley & meat for tea

(about 10lb barley & 5lb meat) 100 men

We used to arrive somewhere for the night to find forty or fifty prisoners already camping out, water boiling on a small stove, somebody cooking food over a fire. If their guards had managed to get some food for the company then that was their good luck. 'Sorry, mate, you can't have any. We were here first.' They weren't going to share anything with us. If they had got the best spot, they weren't going to move. We still kept a sharp eye open in case somebody dropped some food or left a scrap. We were careful to keep quiet about any food we had, particularly anything from a Red Cross parcel. That was very precious cargo. I'm not saying I was attacked for it, although I know others were. Everybody was desperately hungry although I think we managed starvation better than many who had been living in better conditions in their camps, receiving regular Red Cross parcels and not having to work 12 hours day on a farm, in a quarry or down a mine.

I'm not sure when it was that I met Tommy Harrington again. I heard a voice one day, 'All right, Charlie?' and I looked up and saw him. We had stopped for a breather somewhere and he was with his group of men.

'Tommy!' I was delighted to see him. 'I can't believe it.'

'How you doing for food?'

'Not too bad. This and that,' and I told him about finding fish heads and geese legs. 'And potatoes,' and I showed him a couple I had in my pocket. 'Want one?'

'I'll swap you a bit of salt,' and he ferreted about inside his coat and took out a twist of paper. 'Here. That'll make 'em tasty.'

And he went off. 'Best of luck.' What an extraordinary coincidence!

Heb has dropped out.

This was a sad loss to us. Down to four. The first time in five years we five pals were apart. Heb was never very strong but he managed to keep going nearly to the end of our ordeal. He suffered from heart trouble although we didn't know it then. It all got too much for him. He had felt unwell for a couple of days but we managed to help him keep going, carrying him between us at one point but it finally got too much for poor Hebby and he collapsed.

Jimmy and I managed to lift our pal onto the cart as his legs had gone. Because it was full up with other fellows we had to lay him on top of them. It was his only chance; we hoped help wasn't too far away. I believe they were dropped off at the next stalag which may have been on the way to Stendal, our next big stop. Heb did make it home but sadly he had a heart attack and died a few months later. When the four of us met up again after the war we always remembered our friend and how he helped to keep us going.

14

Black Biscuits

When I woke each morning I was glad to be alive, to have survived another night and to still have Jimmy, Laurie and Sid by my side. I can't stress enough how important it was to have people who cared about you and looked out for you during those dreadful months on the road. My pals saved my life. We didn't eat the black biscuits, you see.

As the weather got warmer and the countryside and roads dried out, I found walking easier although finding food and a decent place to sleep was still as bad. It was difficult keeping up morale. I felt completely abandoned yet again. I would have felt better if I had known when it would all be over. I suffered a lot from all the uncertainty. The guards were getting worse, losing their tempers and hitting people. As described earlier, my friend Sgt Sargent got his nose broken by one of them who hit him across the face for no apparent reason. Sometimes we settled down in the evening and the guards went off for a while and then reappeared suddenly. They rushed in, shouting '*Raus, Raus*,' and cleared us all outside. We had to stand in the cold for ages before allowing us back in.

> Have seen quite a number of Yanks now
> and they look pretty bad.

New men were joining our group including Poles, French, Belgians and Americans and others. Some told us how their guards had run and off and left them so they went looking for another group to join and found us. We listened to the latest news and they told us where they had been and what they'd seen; many tales of horror. I think we were luckier than most from the sound of things. Prisoners beaten by guards and men caught in bomb blasts; civilians shot trying to help POWs and their bodies left by the road. They had slept in pig sties and horse stalls with hundreds of other men and worked like us to clear roads and railway lines.

Everything was chaotic. We knew the war was in its final stages but it didn't feel like it; we were caught slap bang in the middle. I knew it could still end badly. I could be killed by a British or American bomber; get a bullet through my head from one of the crazy German guards. Or caught in crossfire and shot by a member of the Red Army.

Yanks billet bombed

About this time we saw small planes going over dropping propaganda leaflets like a sudden shower of giant snowflakes. They were in many languages, saying things like 'For you this war is over' and telling people to surrender. I wish they had dropped some food parcels for us instead.

Working on bombed area (station) cleaning up.
Two more of our men passed away

We arrived on the outskirts of Stendal, a city half way between Hannover and Berlin, a few days after an intense period of Allied bombing. There were houses and factory buildings half-damaged, others in complete ruin. Roads were blocked with debris and overturned vehicles. There was a suffocating damp smell of sulphur hanging in the air. We marched on – this long, straggly line of dirty, dishevelled, crippled men with a cart clattering along behind; we were lucky still to have one. You could hear the sound of our boots crunching over the ground covered in layers of smashed stones, broken glass and brick dust. There were people bent over, picking through the rubble or trying to clear path ways but they didn't even bother to look up when they heard us approaching.

This didn't look at all promising. Was there any safe place to stay? Where would we find anything to eat? We were approaching yet another bombed-out building when the guards signalled us to stop. They went off to take a look round the factory site with its smashed windows and damaged roof. When they came back they herded us towards the rear section which was reasonably intact. I kept an eye on what was left of the roof while checking where I put my feet on broken glass and twisted bits of metal.

We picked our way through the rubble and found a decent spot to settle in. The place looked as though it had been used as a shelter before as there were the remains of fires and rubbish lying around. Nothing there to eat – we checked. The guards went off as usual to see what was going on and look for food. I hoped we were going stay for a few days so we could have a good rest and get back our strength. We were exhausted after another long day walking. Once we sat down we really didn't want to get up again.

About half an hour later the guards came running in shouting, '*Raus. Raus,*' – out, out. Oh, no, not again. Up to their nasty tricks. Why couldn't they leave us in peace? We struggled onto our feet and limped back outside. We were marched at gunpoint in the dusky twilight about half a mile away to the railway station. There was a lot going on there as German soldiers, locals and prisoners were busy clearing bricks, stones and timbers from a recently bombed area.

Then those familiar words: '*Schnell, schnell!*' – quick, quick, '*Arbeiten*!' – work, as the guards prodded us with their rifles. We went off in various directions to join groups here and there, moving piles of rubble and clearing the tracks. It reminded me of the quarry as I picked up stones and bricks with my bare hands to pass along a line of men to waiting trucks in the sidings. An hour or two later as it got too dark to work, a whistle blew and we stopped and I followed everybody away from the station. We lined up in a square and got a bit of bread and some soup from the back of a van. We slept well that night back in our factory billet.

Worked carried on the next day. We marched out again, passing the railway station where the clearance work was still going on and continued further along the line. '*Schnell! Schnell!*' again, and as we rounded a bend, we saw ahead what had happened. A train had derailed and its engine and cattle trucks were lying on their side with one upside down. It was probably transporting supplies because the doors had slid apart and it was full of cardboard boxes, the size of a small shoe box, many spilling out onto the tracks.

Some of the boxes were open and we could see hundreds of these jet black biscuits identical to Spratt's dog biscuits, inside and scattered along the tracks. We didn't know what they were. Some men grabbed some and stuffed them into their pockets, presumably to keep for later.

As we helped to clear the boxes and dump them at the side of the line, we looked more closely at the biscuits.

'What d'you think, Jimmy?' Sid asked.

'Don't touch 'em.'

'Why not?'

'Just look at them,' said Laurie. 'They're all black. Horrible.'

'I've eaten charcoal biscuits,' said Sid. 'They were black and horrible but they got rid of my wind.'

'We've eaten worse,' I said. I didn't like the look of them either but I was starving and was tempted.

'No. Not worth the risk. Could be anything,' Jimmy said. So that was it. Jimmy knew best.

We had no idea what they were made from or their intended use and we agreed not to touch them, however hungry we were. If I had been on my own like some of the other chaps, the loners or those with only one mate to look out for them, then perhaps I would have tried one. Just one, to see what it tasted like. But I didn't. Common sense prevailed. We hadn't come this far to go and do something stupid now.

Because when we woke the next morning we found five of our men had passed away in the night. We knew it was the biscuits. I hadn't heard a thing but others said they had been disturbed by noises, the sound of somebody retching and vomiting. Two of the dead were friends from our company, one the vicar's son who had stood next but one to me in the back row of the camp photo. What a waste!

After another day's work we were on the move again. Before we left we had the chance to bury our two chaps and help bury another nearby. The other two men had to be left behind where they died. Laurie and I managed to get hold of a fork and spade and we dug two shallow graves as best we could in a woody area just near the road. The dead men still wore their identity dog tags round their necks so Sid broke each one in two, took one half and left the other with the body. We lifted our friends into the graves and covered them with earth and rubble. With each spade full of soil we prayed for their souls to rest in peace; and silently thanked our lucky stars for being alive.

We were sad leaving our comrades behind. Sid carried those dog tags back home with him and sent them on to the War Office.

Not long after this, Sid collapsed.

* * *

It was about this time, at my lowest point, that I sat down one night and wrote my *God Help Us* letter about all the things that had happened to us since leaving our camp. Sid had been taken off to one of the stalags nearby and we were now just three – Jimmy, Laurie and me. Who would be next? All I could hear were sirens wailing, planes droning and the sound of not so distant explosions. I felt the ground trembling under my feet. Was this it? Was this what the end of the world was like? 'God help us,' I said.

Jimmy lent me a stub of pencil and somebody gave me a sheet of lined note paper. We were all really scared and desperate. Would we survive this and get home and see our families? Would I ever see my mother or hold Lily in my arms again? I thought I would probably die out there and not be buried, even in a shallow grave. Perhaps somebody would read my note if they found my body.

It was like putting a message in a bottle and throwing it out to sea. You hope somebody will find it, read it and understand what happened. It was a cry for help but I didn't expect anybody to answer. So I wrote down my thoughts, things that had happened up till then; it wasn't meant to be an accurate record of everything. It's hard to make sense of it all. You're so helpless. You do anything to ease to the pain. If people knew what it was like maybe it would never happen again. No sons, brothers or fathers should have to go through this misery and suffering.

I have quoted parts of this letter before but it ends:

Easter Sunday [1 April 1]

Much worse now. 3 have died. Sid collapsed. Taken to stalag. Rations very poor. We are working. Very, very little chance of Red Cross.

War. News is good. We are all hoping it will finish.

God help us.

I folded it up, placed it inside my testament, the gift from the padre, and put it back in my coat pocket.

Just as we had seen planes overhead dropping leaflets, we saw different ones that night; they were reconnaissance planes going overhead. The sky was lit up and we watched them pass overhead, white clouds descending from them, turning into a silver glittering cascade. Wonderful! They were dropping tin foil strips which blocked radar devices and put off the Germans who were firing at them. Clever and rather beautiful among all that noise and ugliness.

We continued on The March with no end in sight. We didn't know where we were exactly. Everywhere looked the same. Dust, debris and broken people. Places, dates and times of the next events are difficult to remember. There were no signposts to our liberation. It just happened one day, without warning, probably towards the end of April, early May.

We were walking as usual along another endless road to nowhere. I was at the back of the column with Jimmy and Laurie when everybody suddenly stopped walking. It took a few seconds to realise we had come to a standstill. Word came down the line that we were going off the road down into a sand pit.

I was scared. 'God, in heaven!' I said to Jimmy, 'You know what that means,' thinking they were driving us all down there to shoot us.

'Only thing to do is to bury yourself in the sand,' he said.

There was nothing else to do but move slowly on ahead; nobody wanted to go fast. We edged off the road down a sandy bank until the road was higher than us. Everybody was spread out and I couldn't see what was going on. The men near us were panicking and some of the fellows had already started burying themselves in the sand. It was all a confusion. And then it went quiet.

I lay there with my face almost in the sand. The only sound I heard was my own breathing rasping in and out, in and out. Nothing else. Suddenly somebody was shouting. I looked up. Some of our fellows appeared above us on the road, waving and shouting, 'It's all right, they've all gone.' They shouted again, 'It's OK. It's OK.' Laurie, Jimmy and I got to our feet and looked at each other in disbelief.

'What's going on?' I said.

'Only way to find out,' and Jimmy started scrambling back onto the road and Laurie and I followed.

'Hey, look at that.' There were abandoned rifles on the ground and two machine guns lying in the middle of the road. Not a single German guard to be seen. They had vanished. I stood looking around me, confused rather than elated at this sudden turn of events. I heard the sound of an engine and turned to see what was coming down the road. God, what now? Should I grab a machine gun and get ready to defend myself rather than just stand there like a sitting duck? I didn't have the energy to do anything but wait and see what it was.

An American jeep drew up with a squeal of tyres beside the men up ahead. Three officers in a four-seater started talking to our chaps and gesturing down the road. Word came back down to us, 'Keep on up the road and you'll meet their company.'

So that was it. The end had finally come. Just like that. The Germans ran off and left us behind. The Americans arrived and took charge.

I remember some things so clearly and odd details are fixed in my mind for ever but the rest – well, it was all a long time ago. I didn't feel any great sense of relief; I was too stunned to say anything. I had kept going for so long and now all I wanted to do was lie down in the middle of the road and never get up. Jimmy put a hand on my shoulder and pushed me gently forward. 'Come on, Charlie. We're nearly there.' I forced myself to go on even though my legs were about to give way. Laurie was in a bad way, too, so we held on to each other and limped along behind the others. 'Nearly there. Nearly there.'

As we made our way that last mile I could see we were heading for some sort of military base. There was a sea of men in fields either side behind the perimeter fence. German prisoners were one side and the British, and everybody else, on the other. I think we had arrived at a German Air Force base, now under the authority of the United States Army Air Force. I looked up and saw planes circling overhead waiting to land. As we entered the gates there were lots of American service men rushing about directing people as they were brought in on foot and by truck. There were able-bodied, walking wounded and sick men on make-shift stretchers everywhere.

People came out to help us and we moved towards the entrance to a large three-storey building. I remember there was a wide staircase inside and some of our group were being led to the upper floors. There were rows of men everywhere lying on the bare floor, on blankets and overcoats. Pale faced boys with dead eyes looked up at me. Laurie and I couldn't walk any further and we stayed at the bottom of the stairs. We saw a space and helped each other towards it, stepping over and around other men. Once I stopped walking, I collapsed in a heap. That was it. My legs had finally given up.

I felt myself sinking like a deep-sea diver underwater. Waves of pain swept over me in every bone and every muscle in my body. I just sank down and down into a sort of semi-conscious state. I was asleep, aware of every sound and movement, but unable to move. I was physically and mentally exhausted and I knew I was safe. Somebody else was responsible for me now. I didn't have to worry about anything ever again.

We stayed there a week or so, I think, maybe longer. I wasn't in any fit state to count the days. People were coming and going around me all the time. I heard voices, felt hands, tasted food. To be honest, there were so many of us there in need of help all they could do was keep us dry and fed and then move us out as quickly as possible. I remember an American woman feeding me bits of white bread, so soft in my mouth, like eating cake and there were tiny biscuits which just dissolved on my tongue. Like baby food; and that's what I was – a baby being fed by its mother.

When I was stronger I was able to get up and have a wash, which was pretty basic but better than nothing. I think I must have borrowed a razor because I had my first shave for four months, I looked in the mirror over the basin and saw this tired old man looking back at me. I was glad my mother couldn't see me now. A stinking, flea-bitten, lice-ridden bundle of skin and bones. A walking skeleton. I was ashamed of myself and what I had become. What would people think? I dreaded being seen like this by anybody who knew me.

As for Lily, I thought it would be better if she married one of her dancing partners. I knew she had men friends and been out with some of them; she had told me so in her letters. I wouldn't hold her to any promises we made before the war. What had I done during five years of war? I wasn't returning a hero. I didn't have any medals to show or tales of bravery to tell. I had nothing to offer. I was a rag and bone man fit only for the rubbish heap.

But I wanted to go home more than anything. Men were on the move all around. There was noise and activity day and night, lights flashing, planes landing and taking off and vehicles coming and going. It would be my turn soon. It must have been a nightmare for the Americans to sort it all out. French and Dutch companies were being dispatched home and I remember a fellow Brit next to me complaining, 'We should be going home before them Frogs.'

It was 8 May, 1945, my 26th birthday, and how did I celebrate? I climbed half way up an American tank so I could hear Churchill's Victory in Europe speech on the tank radio. VE Day. I will never forget it. What a wonderful birthday present!

I was still very weak and somebody gave me a lift up so I could get closer to the set to listen. How wonderful to hear our Prime Minister announce, 'The German war is therefore at an end' and for somebody to thank us for what we had done, 'Our gratitude to our splendid Allies goes forth from all our hearts in this Island and throughout the British Empire.'

A big cheer went up when Churchill mentioned the United States and their 'overwhelming power and resources'. And when I heard, 'Finally almost the whole world was combined against the evil-doers, who are now prostrate before us,' I cried. I was glad that I was no longer a slave and had to prostrate myself before the enemy.

Eventually a load of us, including Laurie and me (I don't know what happened to Jimmy) were moved by truck to an airfield just outside Berlin. We were going home via Brussels. We boarded a Dakota which normally carried parachutists so there were no conventional seats. About 50 of us had to perch on these wooden benches each side of the plane. We landed at Brussels and I expected we would get a shower and some decent food but we didn't. All we had were thin cucumber sandwiches on white bread, and a couple of hours kip sitting on benches in a waiting area.

Early next morning Laurie and I boarded a Lancaster bomber for the last leg of our journey. Comfort rating – zero stars. This time there was a steel bar to sit on in the body of the plane for over 2½ hours. The noise was dreadful. The crew were Australians. Nice fellows. Laurie was put up front in the cockpit, as he was short, next to the navigator who was keen on giving us a running commentary. He wanted us to know what places we were going over, what altitude we were doing and our ETA. As it was so noisy he told Laurie the information and got him to write it down on bits of paper, which were passed back to us to read. That was good. We cheered when we heard we had just gone over the Romney Marshes and Lydd. I'm afraid Laurie and I were still in our old uniforms (same filth, fleas and lice) and I was scratching, Laurie was scratching and I expect everybody else was, including the Aussie crew, by the end of the flight.

We landed at Horsham – back on familiar territory. Not much had changed since I had been stationed there a lifetime ago when I was a fresh-faced young conscript. As we descended from the aircraft and walked off the tarmac onto the field, some of the chaps got down on their hands and knees and kissed the grass. Back on English soil. I didn't do it; I couldn't see the point. All that mattered to me was to get back to Barking to see the family as soon as possible.

We were desperate to go home and hoped that we would have a proper clean up and get through the paperwork for our repatriation as soon as possible. It wasn't asking much was it, after all we had been through. No delays, please. I thought I might still be able to make it home in time for tea and surprise everybody. I hadn't a clue what my family knew about my whereabouts. Even if there was a bit of a delay and I arrived at midnight, I didn't care and I didn't suppose my family would either.

We were escorted to the camp buildings, a group of huts including admin, canteen and some of the officers' quarters. I expected some sort of welcome home. It is hard to believe now how we were treated. I am furious to this day, thinking about it. Nobody seemed to have a clue about us and what we had been through.

I don't remember how many of us had landed at the camp but I do remember that it was a Friday afternoon. Why do I remember this? Because the office personnel who were mostly civilians said, 'I'm sorry but we can't deal with you now. We don't work weekends.' I couldn't believe it. We all protested but they wouldn't budge: 'We'll see you Monday morning. And then you'll be on your way.'

What a way to treat men returning from war. I wondered what their war had been like; pretty cushy, I imagined, compared to ours. They refused to stay in spite of our pleas to make an exception for us. 'No exceptions.' So that was it. We had no paperwork, no travel warrants, no telegrams to send home. Nothing. They wouldn't wait to process us so we could get home as soon as possible. Five years I had waited. Some of the lads just walked out.

They were so desperate that they started walking home but they didn't get far and they returned later as they had no money.

Nobody had any kind words for us, just directions to a tent. 'Take a blanket and your bed,' they said. Oh, no, not those bloody biscuits again. The very same canvas cushions I had slept on five years back in the furniture store in East Grinstead where my army career had started. What did we get to eat? A couple of slices of bread and marge and some lukewarm soup. No change there.

We hung around all weekend until the office opened again on Monday morning. We went to the Quartermaster's store, which was packed to the roof with uniforms of all shapes and sizes. They must have been dealing with a huge number of returning soldiers as the shelves were well stocked. We had showers, threw all our old clothes away, including underwear (what was left) and put on our new uniforms which we had been issued with. Mine didn't fit; everything hung loose on me as I had no arms or legs to speak of. Now I was ready to face the world again.

I was sorry to say goodbye to my mother's boots but they were worn out. Not surprising considering what they had been through. The new ones may have been smart but they were hard on my poor feet which were still in a bad way. It seemed incredible at the time to have all this new stuff when we were going home but, of course, we were still in the army and serving soldiers. I had quite a while to wait until I was officially demobbed.

At last we were dealt with and I signed papers, ticked boxes and sent my field telegram. That was funny because mine arrived about an hour and a half after I did. We were given travel warrants for use on the railway but not on the buses so if your home wasn't near the station, you would have to walk or hope that somebody would give you a lift. We weren't given so much as a penny to put in our pocket.

When I eventually got home to Movers Lane, I found my parents had moved. Some homecoming.

15

Back to Life

'What's two or three miles more to a man who's walked over a thousand?' you might be thinking but I didn't want to walk a step further than I had to. I wanted to go straight home to Barking but the Corporal issuing the travel passes said, 'Ilford Station is the best I can do. Not far to walk, mate.'

I stood on the edge of the kerb outside the station looking for a tram. Traffic whizzed by so fast that I was frightened to cross the road. I was looking for a tram but I didn't know that they had been replaced by trolley buses. I saw one on the other side of Broadway gliding by with 'Barking' written on the back. Damn it! I could have been on that and been home in a jiffy. So I plucked up the courage to cross, dodging between cars, vans and bicycles. The stop was a few hundred yards away and I decided to wait for the next one.

A bus drew up and the conductor was hanging off the rail at the back. As I got on, swinging my kit bag on ahead, he said, 'Steady on, mate,' and ducked.

'I'm sorry but I haven't got any money,' I said, showing him my travel warrant.

'Not valid on this, mate. Sorry.'

I thought he was going to refuse to take me. I told him who I was and where I had come from and just enough about my long journey back across Germany for him to take pity on me. He picked my bag up, put it on a seat inside and said, 'You get in and sit there. Nobody's going to turn you off.'

When we got to Barking station he helped me off, carrying my bag across the road and put it down against a wall. He shook my hand and said, 'Cor! Haven't I got something to tell my missus when I get home.'

I started walking, taking in familiar sights: the junction at Ripple Road, pubs, shops and the Park. I had imagined walking down Movers Lane many times over the last five years. I passed a woman I knew who was sweeping the front step. She looked up but she didn't recognise me. All she said was, 'Oh, another one home.' And I said, 'Yes,' and walked on.

When I got to our little row of shops with the newsagents, grocers, our greengrocers and my aunt and uncle's butchers, I was expecting (or hoping) to see all the family out in the street waiting for me. A bit of a welcome home. Of course, when I got nearer and saw the blinds down in the shops and the closed signs up, I remembered that it was Monday and they didn't open. What a pity! They had probably gone out for the day somewhere and missed my telegram. I knocked on the door just in case but there was nobody home. I wasn't worried so I tried next door at Auntie Elsie and Uncle Joe's.

Their shop was shut but I tapped on the little glass window in the front door and after a few minutes I heard footsteps. The door opened and Auntie stood there, looking at this strange man in uniform on her front step. Then the penny dropped and she just stood with her mouth open, speechless.

'Yes, it is me, Auntie Elsie. It's Charlie,' I stood outside holding my kit bag.

'Who is it?' Joe called out from the back.

Elsie still hadn't spoken to me but shouted back, 'It's Charlie. Alice's boy, come home.'

'Well, don't leave him standing on the doorstep, woman,' Joe shouted from the back. 'Bring him in.' He appeared in the hall in his shirt sleeves and no collar. 'Come on in, lad. Come on in,' and he put his hand out and shook mine so hard I felt my poor bones cracking.

I followed them into the back parlour where three of my girl cousins were sitting at the table. Of course they had changed a bit since I had last seen them, as had I.

'Look who's here, girls. It's your cousin Charlie.' Gwen and Joyce, the older ones, got up and came round to give me a hug. Little Jean followed; she'd been just a toddler when I had last seen her.

'When will they be back?' I said, indicating next door.

'Your parents. Didn't you know? They moved out to Leigh-on-Sea,' Joe said.

'Bought a house. Your dad still works in the shop,' said Elsie.

I told them I hadn't received any letters for at least six months so was out of touch with the family.

'Never mind that. What about something to eat?' Joe rubbed his hands together. 'You look as though you could do with a good square meal inside you.'

I nodded. 'I could eat a horse,' I said.

Joe laughed. 'Sorry, no horse but I could do a nice rump steak or some tasty sausages. What you fancy for your tea?'

My mouth was watering. 'A pork chop, please. That would go down a treat,' I said and Joe went off next door.

Elsie put the kettle on in the kitchen and the girls kept me company. It was lovely to hear their girlish chatter and giggles. Joe went into his cold storage room to check what he had and came back with two enormous pork chops, lovely and pink with a thick ribbon of fat on the side of each one. Sadly, I only managed to eat a couple of mouthfuls. I wasn't used to eating meat or anything much really, and my poor stomach couldn't take it – or my teeth. I had to be careful what I ate for a very long time.

What happened next was that Joe rang one of my brothers with the good news of my safe arrival home and asked him to come round and pick me up and take me to Leigh. All I remember is that on the way there I was looking out of the window taking in everything. We stopped at some crossroads and right on the corner was a big dairy company shop and I could see the window display with a huge cheese on a stand in the middle.

I said, 'Cor, look at that! There's us been crying out for food all this time and you've got cheeses the size of a house.' But you know what, it was a dummy and there wasn't much real cheese around anywhere. Everybody at home was struggling with a ration of 50gms per week, and there I was one night, 1000 miles away, stuffing my face with huge chunks of cheese stolen from the railway truck and a load of horrible rats eating the rest.

We reached my parents' home which was a fine mid-terraced house in what was known as 'the good part' of town. When my mother opened the door and saw me she was lost for words. She wrapped me in her arms and held me tight for a very long time. My father shook my hand, patted me on the back and took me into the front parlour. When my sister Elsie saw me she burst into tears and ran out of the room.

* * *

Lily and I were reunited on the platform at Leigh-on-Sea railway station. I nearly missed her getting off the train as I didn't recognise her in uniform. She was given compassionate leave and had come straight from Slough where she was stationed. She was about to be made a sergeant in the Auxiliary Territorial Service (ATS). Her third stripe was waiting in the office for her to collect and sew on her uniform, when I re-appeared.

Lily made a life of her own while I was away, working to support herself and be independent. She wrote to me and told me about what she was up to so I knew a bit about her work. She was always a hard worker and a year or so after the war broke out she left her job as a seamstress and applied for war work. She was a fitter at a Spitfire factory out somewhere in Hertfordshire, fixing fire guards (special protective windscreens) to cockpits. They were designed to help protect pilots from the serious burns which many suffered when their planes were shot down. That was a good thing to do. Always clever with her hands, my Lily.

She joined the ATS in May 1943 and soon after was promoted to Corporal and put in charge of a whole hut of women. She was involved in training girls for their various jobs in supporting the work of the army.

She learned to drive on a little Austin motor and became a staff driver. She took officers out to meetings just like me in France. She was so well thought of that one of the officers said that she could come and work for her after the war. And now I had come back to spoil everything.

Lily didn't run away in horror when she saw me. She rushed towards me and we fell into each other's arms. We hugged and kissed and that was it. She said nothing about how awful I looked or how thin I was. She didn't say that she didn't love me any more and didn't want to marry me because she had met somebody else. She just said, 'Oh, Charlie,' and looked at me with her big brown eyes and smiled her lovely smile, 'I've missed you so much.'

Three weeks later I took her to a branch of Herbert Wolf, the jewellers, in Oxford Street and bought her the biggest engagement ring I could afford. Buying Lily a ring meant a lot to me. I had always felt guilty about the gold signet ring my mother had given me, which I had exchanged for half of loaf of bread with a German guard. A ring is a powerful symbol of love. Once I put the ring on Lily's finger, I hoped she would never take it off.

I have the receipt in front of me dated 13 June: 'Diamond cluster ring (18ct) £38/10/-.' That was a tidy sum back in 1945 (£1000 in today's money) but only the best for my dear Lily who had waited so long for me. Thanks to my army pay being paid into my bank all those years, and my mother returning the money I had transferred to her account from the camp, I didn't have to borrow money from anybody.

And that was how it was to be all our married life, our 63 years together. Lily and I made our way in the world together without help from anybody.

When the family turned their backs on me – well, you know what families can be like, I had to look after myself. What is it that most families fall out over? Money. And my family was no different. I had been promised various things by my parents such as a car when I came home, but more importantly, to take over the family business. In the end I got neither and was pushed out. Completely. I did feel it was wrong. I had been away for five years and missed out on everything. Everybody else had jobs and their own houses and families; I was starting from scratch and had to make my own way. Left behind again.

When my parents died a few years later, my brothers and sisters suggested we took it in turns to have Elsie, our invalid sister, to stay for two or three weeks at a time. I told them that I wasn't willing to take my turn. Lily and I hadn't been married long and we wanted to be on our own with our young son Brian. We agreed that I would offer one of my brothers a sum of money to take my turn, quite a substantial amount it was. He said 'Yes' to begin with. Unfortunately he was pressured by the others not to accept it even though he could have done with the money. So the family stopped speaking to me. How about that!

The funny thing is that Elsie would probably have been better off if we had all chipped in to support her in a little flat on her own somewhere to give her some independence. Years later some agreed that it would have been a better idea. Although in the end she did hold down a job as an auxiliary nurse and she married when she was fifty to a widower. Sadly she died a few years later.

No point in dwelling on these things. Water under the bridge. Pity that everybody takes sides in family disputes and goes along with the majority. All the hardships I faced on my return made me a stronger person and made Lily and I determined to do things our way and make up for lost time.

We got married on 25 June 1945 in a registry office and my eldest sister Marjorie and her husband Stan Wood were our witnesses. We walked from the registry office in Stratford East along Broadway to Lyons Corner House where we had tea and cakes. That was our wedding reception. Then we went back home which was Lily's parents' flat in a tenement block in West Ham. It had stone steps all the way up and a lift which smelt of urine and rarely worked.

It was a quiet ceremony for obvious reasons. I told Lily that I couldn't face a church wedding with everybody there. I was a bundle of nerves and just wanted to hide away, not stand up in front of a whole church full of people. Lily understood. 'If that's what you want then that's fine by me.' She was wonderful over that.

I'll tell you something fantastic. After we had posed for our wedding photograph, the chap came up to me and said, 'It's entirely up to you but I can make you look better.' I didn't understand what he meant. 'I can fill you out, improve your appearance. Leave it to me.' And so I did. He was being polite because I looked a fright with my sunken eyes and hollow cheeks. I don't know how he re-touched the photo but he did. He puffed up my face so you wouldn't know that I had lost 2 stone and was suffering from malnutrition. So there I am, looking healthy and happy in my wedding photo.

I was looking forward to my first Christmas at home for five years and enjoying it with my new wife. Even though I had been automatically transferred to the Army Reserves, I was surprised to receive a letter from the War Office instructing me to report to Portsmouth Station for postal duties. How could they do this to me? It would mean being away from home again for months including Christmas. There was nothing I could do about it but go.

I went down by train and met other chaps like me on the way there. We talked about how unfair it was to be called up again; how nobody knew or cared about us and what we had been through. We were all quite angry. There were about forty of us in the end and we got more and more angry about the situation as we waited to report for duty.

By the time the Post Office officials arrived, we had decided that we wouldn't do the work. We agreed that it had to be all or nothing. It was no good one man saying, 'OK, I'll do it'; that would spoil it. So we all refused. The PO officials were worried and didn't know what to do. They told us that we had to stay there while they went away to contact their superiors, presumably at the War Office. A while later they returned and told us we had to remain in the station until somebody came down from London the next day. There didn't seem anything else to do but wait and see what they said. We were all used to hanging around like this and kipping down in odd spaces and corners and we did as we were told. I slept on a bench in one of the waiting rooms with my kit bag under my head as a pillow.

The next day when an officer arrived and spoke to us, we were still determined not to work and we refused again. The fellow just said, 'OK' and we went back home. And we got away with it. So I spent Christmas at home after all. However, come the New Year, January 1946, blow me, if I didn't receive call-up papers again. God knows what they thought I was fit for! Well, I found out a few weeks later when I reported to Gravesend Barracks.

You only had to take a look at me to see I wasn't A1. I couldn't walk properly as I had problems with one of my legs and I was still underweight, and a puff of wind would have blown me away. I had a medical and was classified B2 which was 'not fit for normal army duties'. So what duties did the CO order me to do? I had to go around the barracks picking up litter with a stick with a spike on the end. I had to clean windows (only on the ground floor as I couldn't climb a ladder) and wash floors. Not only was it unnecessary as the place was always spotless but it was dreadfully boring and a waste of my time. I had no education, no training or anything during that time. I slept in a dormitory with a load of other men who were as bored as I was and I only went out of the barracks when I had a weekend pass to go home to see Lily. There were other POWs in there who felt like me: this was another prison sentence. Six months I spent there. Totally wrong.

After I got married, I was doing odd jobs for my family, mostly driving around fetching and carrying for the business. I worked for a while for my mother's brother who was a farmer. He didn't own any land but he bought the field crops and employed people to pick them and then take the vegetables to market. Does this sound familiar to you? I helped him with a bit of everything including picking and driving vans full of vegetables to Stratford Market to be sold. It looked as though I had come full circle – back where I started.

When I was transferred to the Army Reserve list, I was issued with my de-mob suit courtesy of the Central Ordnance Depot, Branston (where the pickle comes from). I chose a double-breasted suit in a pin stripe material. I was thrilled to get it, not just in anticipation of finally leaving the army but because I had never had a proper suit. I was particularly pleased to have it when my pal Laurie Neville invited me to his wedding and asked me to be his best man. I wasn't going to let him down. Come to think of it, he was in his de-mob suit too. His wedding was a small family affair and like me he had found a good woman to set up home with.

What Lily and I wanted most of all was a home of our own. We had a roof over our head, moving a couple of times over the next few years. We lived in a rented flat over my brother's shop and then in a rented house with a little garden my brother found us when he sold his shop. It wasn't the same as having our own place. I wanted to find a proper job and be my own boss and save up for a house. I was still a gofer, I think they call it, at everybody's beck and call. No dignity in that. But I wasn't trained in anything; this didn't help me settle back into civvy street.

I have to say that I wasn't an easy person to live with. I got upset very quickly over the smallest thing. I was extremely nervous and didn't like meeting people or being in a crowd; I was afraid of doing some of the simplest tasks. My father got angry with me on one occasion because I wouldn't go and get some petrol coupons for his van from the Town Hall. All I had to do was get a form and fill it in to request a few extra gallons but I couldn't face going out and having to talk to strangers. He kept on about it and told me off for not going, which I resented very much. I was a grown man, not the young lad I had been before the war. So that made me very angry. In the end Lily came with me to the Town Hall but my father should have understood.

I didn't like authority figures before the war and I certainly didn't like them after. So being told off or told what to do didn't go down well with me. I liked being free to do things my way and sometimes when I got frustrated or people crossed me I was not very agreeable. There were times when I did behave badly. I was horrible. I would just explode for no apparent reason and shout and swear at whoever was near – usually Lily, I'm afraid.

When Brian was much older, he told me that I ought to sort this out as it was causing a lot of upset at home. I knew Lily understood but it wasn't nice. You shouldn't take it out on your family but I couldn't help it. It was like a huge build-up of anger and frustration and it had to be released. I couldn't stop. I never talked about the war and I think that had a lot to do with it. Lily did encourage me to talk about what had happened during the war, hoping to find the reason for my behaviour but I didn't tell her. Today I would have had some counselling.

I wish I had talked to somebody about my years as a prisoner, especially about the terrible things I saw. They are as clear today as they were the day I stood by and watched a woman shot in the head; a man beaten to death with a spade and left in a bloody heap by the road. It wouldn't have been fair on Lily to burden her with all that. The constant fear I felt, my sense of shame at my degradation and my helplessness to do anything about what I saw. These feelings affected me deeply. I was so disgusted by the way the Germans behaved that I wanted to blow the whole lot of them to smithereens. I was so angry and carried that hatred inside for a long time.

One of the best times was when Lily and I set up our own greengrocery round from the back of a lorry. Brian was born in 1946 and had started school so this was probably in the early 1950s. It was hard work with long hours but we were our own bosses and enjoyed being together. It wasn't a deliberate act to set myself up in opposition to the family business; it just sort of happened that way.

A friend of mine who knew I was looking for work had heard about some second-hand removal vans for sale. A firm which made cough mixture – I forget the name, had gone out of business and were selling off their vehicles, including these 2-ton delivery lorries. He thought that one of those would make a nice shop and offered to show me them. He took me down to a garage in Deptford where five were displayed on the forecourt. He knew a bit about engines and looked them over and listened to them running and he picked the best one out for me. I made an offer to the salesman and I bought it for £100 on credit over five years.

My nephews, Keith and Roy, had inherited their father's carpentry skills and they came and helped me fit out shelving inside. I hadn't fallen out with my big brother Alfred but he didn't want to upset other members of the family so I rarely saw him. That was a pity. We got the inside all ship shape and I set out all the different bins for the vegetables (just like in the old shop) and stocked them up and it really looked the business.

I decided to stick to a familiar district and people I knew and set up round the corner from my old home and family shop. I gradually built up my own customers and expanded the route. I had a very loyal following and some of my old ones started coming to me instead of the shop. I've always got on with people in spite of being shy and if you provide a good service to the public, they trust you and you can do well. I suppose there was the idea at the back of my mind that I might get sympathy from people who knew me from the old days, who thought I had been treated badly by my relations.

And yes, I did take business away from the family and yes, they didn't like it and tried to stop me. Somebody reported me to the council saying I was breaking the law by selling goods from a stationary vehicle in the street. So when an official came and spoke to me about it, all I did was to get in the driving seat of the van and move it a few feet further down the road. Then I decided to check with the police and went down to the station. They told me that they hadn't received any complaints so I could carry on. Word soon got back after that: not to bother Charlie again.

We did have fun together and Lily got on with all the customers and I didn't mind chatting to them either because I knew them and wanted to please them. Over time, the weekly takings got better and better and I am proud to say that we were very successful.

After a few years of the greengrocer's round I decided it was time for a change. What I needed was a job with regular hours and regular pay. It wasn't fair on Lily being stuck with me all day in the back of a van or on Brian who didn't see much of us. We both wanted to enjoy a proper family life while Brain was growing up. Lily also wanted to broaden her horizons and had an eye on working again using her sewing skills.

She soon found work in a clothing factory owned by singer Sandie Shaw's father out in Hainault, I think it was. She took Brian to school before work and picked him up after. Then she went on to work for a large furniture manufacturer where she learned to do upholstery and became very skilled in that specialist work. She continued making her own clothes in her spare time and made all Brian's when he was little. He was always perfectly turned out, whatever the occasion.

One day Lily and Brian, who was four years old at the time, were in Dolcis Shoe Shop in Romford. Lily was looking for new shoes for Brian and he caught the eye of a photographer who was doing some advertising work there. He was setting up a shot and thought Brian would look good in it. Brian had to sit next this glamorous model and look on as she tried on shoes. He looks angelic in his beret and best tailored coat, another of Lily's creations. It's a lovely picture and appeared in several magazines.

What about me, then? What was I going to do with myself? All I was qualified to do was drive and sell things. And that is what I continued to do in my next job, which lasted twenty-seven years. However, the difference was that this job took me from the bottom rung of the ladder almost to the top.

16

On the Road Again

I nearly didn't get the job at Macarthys Ltd in Romford because of the young girl on the reception desk. 'The advert clearly says, "Drivers between 25–35 required" and you're 39,' she said.

I had seen the advert for drivers in the local paper and thought I would give it a go. I stopped off on my way back from market with a lorry load of potatoes. I went in and filled in a form with my personal details and passed it over to the girl. When she saw my date of birth she pushed the paper back to me.

'I'm sorry. It's no good me passing it on upstairs. They won't even look at it. You're too old.' That was it and I left and went back to deliver my spuds. I persisted however and some days later I started working for a company which grew from small beginnings, from working out of the back of a chemist shop, into one of the country's leading wholesale pharmaceutical distributors.

My first job was accompanying one of the drivers in his 12cwt Bedford van full of surgical dressings which we delivered to the hospital at the Ford Dagenham Works. I suppose I was the spare driver and now I knew what Pony Moore felt like in France when he was sitting in the passenger seat beside me. I accompanied this chap for a few days to learn the ropes and then I was given my own route and left to get on with it. I collected the orders from the warehouse, loaded them up and then went out on my round to the various customers, mostly pharmacists. I was out on the road again, on my own.

I didn't think of myself as just another driver or delivery boy – well, certainly not a boy at nearly forty. I didn't want to be one of those fellows who just dumped the goods out the back and then drove on to the next job. I took an interest in the people I met and spent time chatting to them and tried to be friendly and helpful. If somebody wanted to change or add to an order I would see to it personally. I got myself a notebook and started keeping records of the various requests. I sorted them out myself in the warehouse when I got back. Nothing was too much trouble.

I was doing well and enjoyed what I was doing, particularly offering a more personal service. People told me, including customers and reps from other drugs companies, that I ought to be out on the road selling. 'Got the gift of the gab,' I heard somebody say. 'You're a natural.'

'They don't take drivers off the road and make them reps,' I said.

One day a sales rep from Pfizer was standing on the kerb outside one of my regular customers. As I passed him to go into the chemists, he said hello and started chatting. I had seen him before and didn't know his name but he knew mine.

'Awright, Charlie. How you doing?'

'Fine, thank you,' I said, 'and you?'

'Tickety-boo.'

I thought that was it but he continued, 'Little birdie tells me,' and he tapped the side of his nose, 'Little birdie tells me that a certain person not a million miles from here is coming up in the world.'

I had no idea what he was talking about.

'They're trying to get you out on the road, repping. You know, like yours truly.'

'I don't know what you mean.'

'Your bosses. Haven't you heard?'

I shook my head. 'Don't be ridiculous. I'm a driver.'

But you know what? They did want me out on the road, wanted me to become a sales representative. What's more, I did become one and continued to do so for the next 20 years until I retired in 1984.

Things have happened to me more by accident than intention. I've been lucky. I left school at fourteen without any qualifications but I've done well. People always seemed to take to me and my face fitted. I worked with two regional directors where all the other reps worked with one. They left it up to me to organise my work load which I really appreciated. I remember the first time they called me into their office to tell me the good news.

'You see that desk there.'

'Yes, sir.'

'It's nice and empty.'

'Yes, sir.'

'Well, I want it staying that way. I don't want a load of rubbish on my desk on a Friday afternoon.'

'No, sir.'

'We know where you are and what you're doing. If we want to speak to you we can find you at home, can't we?'

'Yes, any time,' I said.

That was fine by me. There was nobody breathing down my neck and there were no piles of paper to deal with or reports to send in. I was very lucky. I had good bosses who respected and trusted me enough to let me get on with my job.

I was put in charge of part of the South East area: the whole of Essex, part of Hertfordshire and part of Kent. We were living in Thundersley, near Southend, by then, so I was travelling a good deal on my patch but soon got to know all the other places. Sometimes one of my bosses asked me to cover for another rep in a different area if that chap was absent or unavailable.

Most of what I did was what is known as 'cold calling'. I went out and visited chemists, pharmacists and doctors who didn't know me from Adam and didn't buy from us. My job was to sell my company to them and get them to move their accounts from their wholesaler and sign up to us. I wasn't pushy or grasping or greedy. I know some reps would do anything to get a new customer but I treated people with respect and I did very well. Occasionally people closed the door in my face but mostly they were polite and spared me the time to hear what I had to say about the service and competitive prices my company could offer. You did need a bit of a silver tongue and I had that, so it seemed. As my boss said, 'We employ you because you're a good talker.' Funny to think how shy I used to be and how I would go out of my way to avoid meeting people.

When I went out in the morning I was my own boss in my company car, out on the road, not stuck indoors – what I've always liked best. I didn't have to report to anybody or ask for permission to do so and so. I used my initiative in arranging my visits. If I had been on a long journey one day I worked locally the next. If I fancied an afternoon off then I took it and made up the time another day. This suited me and fitted in well with the family. I could be doing a couple of hundred miles a day but I always tried to get home in time for tea.

Family life was important to me. I needed love and security after all those years of hardship and neglect as a POW. It was such a lonely time, even with your pals for company. They had their own fears and worries. Men don't talk about their feelings like women and I kept mine bottled up.

Lily was a wonderful wife and companion and made a lovely home for me. When Brian came along that gave me a real purpose in life and I wanted to be a good father. I never thought I would ever marry and have a child. When I lay on my bunk bed at night in the camp, listening to men snoring and rats gnawing the floorboards, I stopped myself from thinking about Lily and being with her in a place of our own. It was too painful. I honestly believed that I would die out in that dreadful place. One year turned to two, and then three to four, and then five. An eternity of misery.

I had everything I wanted now and life was good; Lily and Brian were settled and happy. However, the time came, as it always does, when the bosses wanted more.

When I first started at Macarthys there were about 400 staff in Romford; by the time I retired in 1984, they had over 4000 and had expanded their premises and locations. There were always new drugs coming on the market and at the beginning they were very expensive because of the cost of the research. I was handling orders worth a hell of a lot of money. The company was doing very well indeed. They could afford to be generous with bonuses for employees but when one of the directors handed me a huge roll of money held together by a rubber band I was taken by surprise.

I was called to the board room one day and the directors told me that they needed somebody to cover the Midlands region. I told them I was happy where I was and turned the offer down and that was it for a while. They asked me a second time and I was worried that if I refused again I might lose my job.

'Mr Moore, tell me, does this mean I'm on the scrap heap?'

'Oh, no, not at all. You carry on with what you're doing.'

So I did. For a bit longer.

Lily knew what was going on. I told her about the meetings and she said, 'We're settled here, aren't we?'

'Yes, we are. I told them I wasn't moving.'

They kept asking me and I kept saying no. It was on the third or fourth occasion that the roll of bank notes appeared. I was sitting opposite the director again when he pushed the money across the desk. 'Have a think about it,' he said.

On that particular day Lily was busy repainting the garage doors when I pulled into our drive just before midday. She only had to look at my face to know what had happened.

'Oh, no, they've asked you again, haven't they?'

'Yes, they had me in the office first thing.' I showed her the bundle of money. 'Look what they gave me.' I'd had a quick look at it in the car and reckoned there was more than £50 in notes (worth over £600 in today's money). I took Lily's hand. 'It's all right, I'm not taking it.'

The next day I returned the money without saying a word. I thought that would the end of it and they would get the message. I don't know why, but they were persistent buggers and the next time they asked me I said yes. It was Lily's decision. I think she realised that they must have thought an awful lot of me the way they kept offering me this and that incentive to move. She thought that a change might be good after all. If you can't beat 'em, join 'em. We moved to Kidderminster in 1972 and I have lived there ever since.

I never wanted an office job or to be a boss or tell people what to do and fortunately that continued. I worked hard finding my way around a different part of the country and slowly built up my business with a whole new lot of customers. The Essex Boy was getting used to Brummie and Black Country ways. Lily and I worked awfully hard in those days and we only took short holidays or had days out. We enjoyed gardening and spent our spare time worked together on our patch at the back. Lily had the ideas and the artistic flair, and designed the layout and chose the plants while I provided the muscle. You know me –good with a fork and spade.

When I retired they held a party for me in the Birmingham depot. I was presented with a carriage clock which sits on my mantelpiece and is still going and keeps good time. Lily received a beautiful bowl of plants and a bouquet. She was very popular and had also worked for a while in one of their depots helping with the daily orders. I left the company at the right time because a year later they were taken over and everything changed. I was lucky.

I think it was about this time that my niece Ann Broom (my second eldest sister Doris's girl) paid me a visit. We got talking about the family and were sharing memories of childhood and growing up.

'What did you do in the war, Uncle Charlie?' she said and asked if she could see my medals.

'What medals?' I said, 'I haven't got any.'

'Of course you do,' she said. 'Everybody who served in the war has them. Even Auntie Lily.'

We had never received our service medals – the 1939–45 Star. In addition I should have had the War Medal 1939–45. I thought we both deserved them considering what we had gone through. Ann found the address for me and I wrote to the MoD Medal Office in Glasgow with our details. A while later a package with a Droitwich post mark arrived. It was only a few miles away where the medals were struck. They came in two little boxes and I thought somebody had sent us some wedding cake. When I opened them there were our medals nestling in tissue paper inside, not a piece of iced fruit cake. I wouldn't have minded that as well.

I didn't have any reason to wear my medals back then but I put them away somewhere safe. I am proud today to wear them on Remembrance Sunday and at any function or occasion I attend where it is appropriate.

There were changes when I retired. I was spending more time with my family which I liked. I was always happiest when it was just the three of us. It was Lily and Brian's turn to do what they wanted and I wanted to support them now their interests. Lily still loved sewing and enjoyed making things for friends. Her aprons and cosmetic purses were very popular and she decided to take a stall at a local craft fair. She was very successful and we started going regularly to these and bigger shows all over the place. I was happy taking a back seat, apart from doing the driving that is. Lily didn't need me to do any selling as her goods just flew off the table by themselves.

Brian spent a lot of his free time on his hobby which was replica model train building. He started showing his models which he made from scratch in his workshop, engineering every piece by hand. He exhibited at model railway clubs and fairs in school halls and at venues like Birmingham's National Exhibition Centre. I accompanied him to his shows and enjoyed helping him set things out and chat to the people who came to look at his exhibits. Not that I knew much about the details, dimensions, gauge etc of the engines. Bit over my head. Being with Lily and Brian kept me busy and out on the road yet again.

Lily and I never travelled abroad. Lily didn't like flying or going on boats so we always holidayed in this country. We never needed passports. However, Brian loved travelling and went all over the world and learned to speak French fluently and a bit of German. I would have loved to learn German. That is one of my regrets from all those years as a POW that I never learned more than a few words and phrases of German. I have tried to learn a bit on my own but it's not easy.

Then in May 2010, at the age of 91, I got my first passport and I went abroad.

* * *

I am looking out over the sea from the top deck of the Cross Channel ferry. This is the second time I have been on my way to France. The first time the only documents I needed were my call-up papers, army pay book and a clean driving licence. His Majesty King George VI waived the need for a passport. Now I am returning in very different company.

The film crew have been very good to me. It's chilly on deck and Peter has a blanket ready to put round me if I feel cold as soon as Nick has finished this bit of filming. I have to look out to sea and look as though I am remembering April 1940 when I boarded the troop ship at Southampton. I don't need to act. The emotions are real. I remember it as though it was yesterday.

Peter Vance and Nick Maddocks from Testimony Films have arranged for me to visit Dunkirk and they will film me walking on the beach where I should have been on 27 June 1940 and probably drowned or been shot to pieces. They are taking me to a road near Abbeville where I am going to retrace the route I took the day my convoy met the German tanks and troops. It won't be the exact spot where I was captured but I am feeling the same goose bumps and cold sweat I felt all those years ago when I was shit-scared facing those hundreds of enemy soldiers.

How wonderful at my age to have new experiences and new memories to store away! My good friends and neighbours Allan Jones and his wife Jan, are travelling with me and Allan has borrowed his son's video recorder and is filming me being filmed. I've never had so much attention since the film company contacted me about taking part in a documentary for the Yesterday Channel called *Dunkirk: The Forgotten Heroes* marking the 70th anniversary of the evacuation from Dunkirk.

How many people get the opportunity to go back and relive important moments in their lives, however painful, to share with others who are interested and also want to learn what it was like? All that has happened to me recently has been amazing. I have good people around me, friends and family who care about me. And that's a wonderful thing to be able to say. This is what keeps me going. I have no Lily and I have no Brian to keep me company any more.

I wouldn't have been on television or have been approached to write a book if Allan hadn't suggested that I join the National ex-Prisoner of War Association (NEXPOWA). He had heard some of my stories about my experiences during the war and he thought it might be good for me to join and meet other people – give me a new interest. He was worried about me because I was in a pretty bad way after I lost Brian in November 2006 followed by Lily, ten months later in August 2007 – as he said, I was going downhill rapidly. I lost a lot of weight and was very withdrawn.

My wife and son were the world to me. They left such a big hole in my life after their deaths that I couldn't see the point of going on. Why I was still alive? It should have been me that died. I had always thought of myself as lucky but my luck had finally run out. I had nothing really to live for – or so I thought.

Through NEXPOWA I met Terry Waite CBE at the Imperial War Museum North. I was representing the Association and Terry was opening the *Captured* exhibition in May 2009. We got on well and were talking so much as he was waiting to go on the platform that he missed his cue and had to be rushed on stage. I was thrilled when Terry Waite agreed to write the Foreword to my book.

The TV documentary brought me a lot of attention. Lots of people saw the programme (and it's still being repeated now) and I was interviewed by newspapers and magazines. This is how Dee La Vardera, a writer from Wiltshire, heard about me and made contact. Allan recorded me on my return trip to France and posted it on You Tube and more people saw that.

I have been to local schools to talk to children and twice visited USAF Lakenheath to address their annual National POW/MIA (Missing Action) Recognition Day. The second time was in September 2010 and I was privileged to be presented with an award from the Air Force Sergeants'

Association Chapter 1669 'with endless gratitude'. I accepted this on behalf all those who didn't return.

I made another trip abroad with Allan in August 2010 to visit Ypres and the Menin Gate. Allan had arranged with The Last Post Association for me to lay a wreath at the evening ceremony. I felt it was a great honour and privilege to do so and I was meant to deliver the oration 'At the going down of the sun and in the morning we shall remember them.' There were nearly a thousand people there and I was so overcome with emotion that I said that I couldn't do it. Fortunately, one of the Standard Bearers from the British Legion stepped in to read it.

After the bugle fanfare, the wreath laying began and it was my turn. The band was playing *The Lord is my Shepherd* and I was near to tears but I managed to cross the road under the Memorial Arch, clutching Allan's arm. I climbed the twelve steps up to the dais and the area where wreaths and tributes are left on three metal shelves. I laid my wreath which was dedicated to 'My fellow POWs who did not make it back from Stalag 20B'. I returned to my wheelchair without breaking down completely.

After the ceremony people came up to shake my hand and thank me; many had read my wreath. One man said, 'Thank you for what you did for Australia,' I really appreciated it. Nobody thanked me at the time. When you think how I was treated after the war it's fantastic today to have people who weren't born until after the war showing their appreciation. You can see the ceremony on You Tube. I don't know who has seen it but it's wonderful to think that people around the world can go online and watch the film clip and remember.

I was also interviewed and filmed by Stephen Saunders from ASA Productions who was working on a film about ex POWs' experiences in prison camps and on the Long March home. The three-part documentary called *The Long March to Freedom* is to be broadcast on UKTV Yesterday in autumn 2011. I am pleased that more people will learn about this neglected part of our wartime history. As the press release says, 'a truly touching and unbelievable story of survival and hope.' Yes, that sums it up well.

My phone has never stopped ringing with family and friends enquiring about what I am doing next. I love talking to people – that's why I was a salesman. And I tell them stories of my war time experiences if they are interested. People kept saying to me, 'You ought to write it all down' and so I have, thanks to the patience and hard work of Dee. Even my hairdresser treats me like a celebrity and says, 'I'll buy a copy when it's out.' I have promised to sign one for him.

I have loved every minute of it. It's got me talking about all the things which I kept hidden for most of my life. Yes, it has made me go over some very painful memories but they only upset me for a short while. I have thought a lot about my old pals and what a help and comfort they were to me during our years together. I remember the good times we had together after the war. Laurie and Sid came over to watch cup finals on my television. Sadly, I lost touch with Sid but remained good friends with Laurie until his death in 1988. His son Robert is my pal now and phones and visits me regularly.

Jimmy Sellar is the only one left. As I described earlier, I drove up to Scotland once to see him in his highland cottage near Inverness. Lily, Brian and I stayed and we ate mutton stew together in their cosy little kitchen. We still exchange cards at Christmas and I ring Jimmy from time to time. I hope that when he reads my book he feels that I have done justice to that part of our lives which we shared.

I am so thrilled that people will be able to read about my life. I am only an ordinary chap from Barking in Essex but I did live through extraordinary times and survived against the odds. A lucky man. I always wanted people to know what had happened to me and other men like me and what we suffered. I want people to remember those who didn't come back but were left behind, buried in shallow graves or left where they fell. I want youngsters to understand about the past so that they don't make the same mistakes as others did.

* * *

I saw some terrible things during the war and I didn't think I would ever see anything else as bad. But watching my son Brian die of cancer was the worst thing to happen to me.

I am glad that my son had a good life and was successful in all the things he loved doing. Lily and I wanted him to have a good education which he did; he went to Liverpool University and studied engineering. We wanted him to have a good job which he did; he became a manager at Severn Trent Water Authority. We were pleased that he followed his dreams which included studying music, playing jazz piano and writing a book. He became a significant figure in the world of model train engineering with his hand-built replicas. He was good at everything he did; he was

Charles at home with his award presented 'With Endless Gratitude' by AFSA Chapter 1669, National POW/MIA Recognition Day, 17 September 2010.

very patient and meticulous, a perfectionist. All his good qualities were certainly inherited from Lily, not from me.

Lily wanted to be a professional singer but her mother had other ideas, so she always encouraged Brian with his music. He used to go up to London to study music with a violinist from the BBC Symphony Orchestra and continued making the two-hour journey every week when he moved back to live with us in Kidderminster. Lily used to travel with Brian to his gigs all over the country and enjoyed hearing him play piano in his jazz trio, Mosaic. He wrote a book, *Modern Jazz Piano: A Study in Harmony and Improvisation*, which is still regarded as the definitive text book on the subject.

Dee with Charles, Kidderminster, May 2011.

My friend Allan entered Brian's name on the search engine on his computer for me and showed me all the entries on my son. There is a marvellous obituary to him on www.gonetoosoon.org and he has 5 star reviews on Amazon for his jazz piano book which still sells in America. That would be good if I could get reviews like him with my book. Goodness, wouldn't Brian and Lily have been proud of me! I wish they were alive to read about my life and the things I couldn't talk about which happened to me during the war.

I never thought I would write a book. Never dreamed it would happen to an ordinary fellow like me. It's been a wonderful experience. I have cried a lot and laughed a lot with Dee as I told her my life story and dug deeper into my past. As we put all my thoughts and memories together down on paper and put them in order, it has been like doing a huge jigsaw puzzle spread out on the dining room table. Lily and Brian loved doing them. Me, I never had the patience.

First you find a few pieces of sky and grass and position them at the corners. You pick out more and put them in the right place and see the picture grow, filling out to meet the edges. You go away and leave it for a while and then come back and try again, adding more and more until you only have the last few pieces in your hand. Where do they fit together to complete the picture? Ah, yes! There and there. It's done – and there's not a piece of the puzzle left behind.

Index

German prisoners of war after their capture near Goch.

German prisoners of war disembark at a British port.

German prisoners of war dig a trench at Shooter's Hill near London, 22 May 1945.

Italian prisoners of war captured near El Alamein are led to the 'cage' by their British guard, 1942. (Library of Congress)

Japanese prisoners of war are led into captivity by US soldiers in the Philippines. (Library of Congress)

Japanese prisoners of war recover from their wounds in US custody in the Philippines. (Library of Congress)

Memories of a Prisoner of War

I find it hard just to explain
As I travel back down memory lane
Of the strength of mind, and stale black bread
And cattle trucks, and frozen dead

The companionship, when might was right
The petty thieving in the night,
The lice, the rags, the hunger pains
The barbed wire fence, the stink of drains

The sudden blackouts when you stand
A raging torrent of commands,
Sleeping in snow in open spaces
Guards death frozen in their places

Sharing out each little mite
Eating potatoes black with blight
Clogs and foot cloths hurting feet
While topping miles of sugar beet

Dreaming of bellies being filled
While just another prisoner's killed,
The eager listening to all news
The lies, the rumours, the different views

The escapes we made through the fence
The movements of freedom, sweet and tense,
The beatings up, the bread and water
That followed on our capture later

Notes of love for everyone
Dear John letters by the score,
Deep despair then face to wall
One prisoner less at morning call

The seething square at roll-call's roar
Forty short or twenty more,
Long hours standing in the rain
A mighty effort keeping sane

The long, long trek to the west
Man's endurance put to the test,
Exhausted stragglers at roadside lie
Mingling with the hordes that die

Burning buildings all around
Aircraft rockets smash the ground,
Your chosen tree it is your fate
Machine gun bullets sing their hate

Fifteen thousand when the march began
But only six when all was done,
Each face still stands out bright and clear
The friends and comrades of yesteryear

Remembering always makes me sad
A blazing world that had gone mad,
Tempering out tolerance of fellow being
Peculiarities were passed unseeing

Perhaps it is not good to dwell
On times when life was simply hell,
God grant we never do repeat
Treating people just like meat.

By Harry Tapley
4th Btn Gordon Highlanders
PoW No. 5532
Kriegsgfangener Lager Stalag XXB, XVIIIB, XXA

By kind permission of Roger Tapley.